WORLD'S
GREATEST
CARD
TRICKS

BOB LONGE

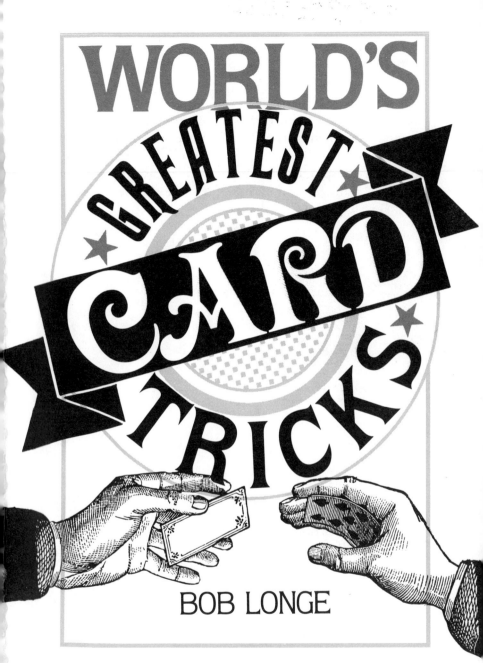

WORLD'S GREATEST CARD TRICKS

BOB LONGE

Sterling Publishing Co., Inc. New York

Dedication

This salute to my good friend Wally Wilson is long overdue. Over the years, he has provided me with a great deal of good material and many useful suggestions. What's more, for decades he has inspired and assisted countless aspiring young magicians, many of whom are highly successful performers today. For all of us, Wally, thanks.

Library of Congress Cataloging-in-Publication Data

Longe, Bob, 1928–
    World's greatest card tricks / Bob Longe.
      p. cm.
    Includes index.
    ISBN 0-8069-5991-6
    1. Card tricks. I. Title.
    GV1549.L536   1996
    795.4'38—dc20   95-46815
                             CIP

3 5 7 9 10 8 6 4 2

Published by Sterling Publishing Company, Inc.
387 Park Avenue South, New York, N.Y. 10016
© 1996 by Bob Longe
Distributed in Canada by Sterling Publishing
% Canadian Manda Group, One Atlantic Avenue, Suite 105
Toronto, Ontario, Canada M6K 3E7
Distributed in Great Britain and Europe by Cassell PLC
Wellington House, l25 Strand, London WC2R 0BB, England
Distributed in Australia by Capricorn Link (Australia) Pty Ltd.
P.O. Box 6651, Baulkham Hills, Business Centre, NSW 2153, Australia
Manufactured in the United States of America
All rights reserved

Sterling ISBN 0-8069-5991-6

Contents

INTRODUCTION

The ability to perform good card tricks is not unlike the gift of playing a musical instrument well. As with a musical instrument, you can enjoy the solitary practice, and you can share your skill with others.

Are there other rewards? Certainly. The admiration of spectators, for instance. Who doesn't enjoy being the center of attention? But even better is the sharing. You, the card expert, enliven every occasion and contribute to everyone's enjoyment.

When performing card tricks, however, some magicians miss the main point. The object is not merely to fool spectators, nor to impress with a variety of flourishes. The object is to *entertain*. And magic is the central theme. The tools are many: good tricks, practised skill, interesting patter, humor, and—above all—a sharing of the fun.

• You have good tricks in this book, some of the best ever invented. And with the deceptive moves provided, every single one is within your grasp. The vast majority, however, require no "sleights"—only practice.
• The practice is up to you. Before performing a trick, you should have every move, every gesture down pat. Work on the misdirection. Make everything seem *natural*. Shakespeare has Hamlet tell the players: "Suit the action to the word, the word to the action; with this special observance, that you o'er-step not the modesty of nature." Good advice for the magician.
• Patter suggestions accompany every trick. You should use only the patter that you're comfortable with. In many in-

stances, you can develop a story line that will suit you much better than anything I could provide.

• Some performers are naturally funny; somehow their every trick evokes appreciative chuckles and outright laughter. Other performers use canned humor. They use memorized lines, most of them borrowed. If you're going to use prepared humor, at least make it original.

• But more important than being funny is an attitude of good humor. Tricks are presented cheerfully. The attitude is this: "We're all here to enjoy ourselves, and I want you folks to join in and contribute to the fun."

Again, the object is to entertain.

Skill with the pasteboards is not enough. Some feel that the card performer should not do *any* flourishes, that to openly display your skill detracts from the "magic" of the tricks. I'm not sure this is true. But I do know that the flourishes can be overdone.

The idea is to entertain an audience, as well as yourself.

Far worse are those boors who believe that knowing how to do card tricks gives them a license to be obnoxious. Not everyone will want to react to these yahoos the way I do. "Here, buddy, take a card!" says Mr. Pretentious Prestidigitator. I do. And walk away with it, saying, "Thanks."

Everyone has a somewhat different way of presenting card tricks. My approach is one of wonderment. "How did that trick work? I'm as puzzled as you are. Maybe *you* made it work; after all, you're the one who cut the deck." Yes, people realize that I'm kidding. But this approach is certainly better than that of the performer who seems to be saying, "Well, I fooled you, again. Boy, are you dumb!"

You'll feel enormously pleased with yourself as you develop greater skill with your tricks, and well you should. Just don't forget to share the joy.

Deceptive Moves

I call this part *Deceptive Moves* because the term *sleights* implies digital dexterity and hours of dreary practice. Clearly, with the moves given here, the more practice the better. But the fact is that they are not difficult. You should strive to make each maneuver look smooth and natural.

Several of the tricks in this book call for a deceptive move or two. Frequently, you have a choice of maneuvers. For instance, in the section *Control,* you have four different methods of bringing a selected card to the top. Included is one of my own invention which has never appeared in print before.

Sometimes it's important to demonstrate that the cards are mixed. So in the section *False Cuts* there are two good ones. Again, one is my discovery and has never before been in print.

Two easy forces are in the section *Forces.*

The *Glide* is a utility sleight which every aspiring card performer should know.

CONTROL

In the first three maneuvers in this section, you quickly bring a card to the top of the deck. In each instance, a card is selected. You fan out the deck for the return of the card. When it is replaced, you get a small break above it with your left little finger as you close up the deck. When you perform the deceptive move, the card is brought to the top of the deck.

Let's suppose that you want the chosen card to be third from the top. When the chosen card is returned, fan two cards on top of it; *then* insert your left little finger as you close up the deck. After the move, the card will be third from the top.

♦ *Double-Cut* ♦

This is probably the most useful control you can learn. It is, in effect, a complete cut of the deck. Therefore, it's good for bringing a card to the top, *or* bottom, or to within a small number of cards from the top or bottom. Furthermore, it's an excellent way to bring a single card (or a small number of cards) from the top to the bottom.

Let's say you're holding a break above the chosen card with your left little finger. Transfer the break to your right thumb so that your palm-down right hand is holding both the deck and the break from above (Illus. 1). With the palm-up left hand, take half of the cards that are below the break and, from the left side, slide them on top. You'll probably have to raise your right first finger to allow passage. Then

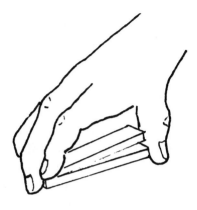

Illus. 1

take the rest of the cards that are below the break and slide them on top in the same way.

The chosen card is on top.

◆ *Easy Control* ◆

Ian Land and I independently arrived at a similar card control. Let's call mine *Easy Control* and his *Even Easier Control.* My method is not a complete cut of the deck, so it is useful only for bringing a chosen card to the top or within a few cards from the top.

You are holding a break above the chosen card with your left little finger. Fan through about half of the cards *that are above the break,* saying, "We know your card is in here somewhere." With your right fingers on the right side, flip this group face up onto the deck. Rapidly fan through these face-up cards, saying, "Could be here." Stop fanning when you get to the first face-down card.

Close up the fanned cards so that they slide into your right hand. Hold this group separate as you continue fanning down to the break held by your left little finger. With the tips of the right fingers flip over the cards you just fanned out so that they are now face up on the balance of the deck.

Here's the situation: In your right hand is a group of face-up cards. On top of the balance of the deck is another group of face-up cards, which you have just flipped over.

As soon as these cards land face up, rapidly fan through them, adding them below the cards in your right hand. Say, "Could be here." Stop fanning when you get to the first face-down card (the chosen card).

Again, loosely close up the fanned cards. Hold them slightly to one side as you flip the remaining cards face up with your left thumb. Add these to the bottom (or rear) of those in your right hand as you fan through them, saying, "Could be here." Stop about two-thirds of the way through, saying, "Who knows?" Close up the entire bunch and turn the deck face down. The chosen card is now on top.

During this last fanning, make sure you do not reveal the lowermost card, which is the one chosen.

♦ *Even Easier Control* ♦

Ian Land's method is similar to mine, but his is a complete cut of the deck. Since the bottom card is revealed during the move, you can't use it to bring a card to the bottom. You *can* use it, however, to bring a card within a small number of cards from the bottom. And it can be used to bring a card to the top or within a small number of cards from the top. I think you'll like the simplicity of this method.

Again, you're holding a break above the chosen card with your left little finger. Turn over the top card of the deck, saying, "Your card is not on top." Replace the card face down.

With the palm-down right hand, grasp all the cards above the break at the left side. Pivot them in an arc to the right, as though opening a book from the back (Illus. 2). "It's not here in the middle."

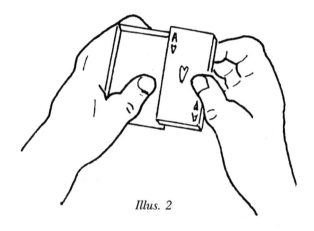

Illus. 2

Move your right hand with its cards a bit to the right. With your left thumb, flip over the cards that are in your left hand, saying, "And not on the bottom."

Place the face-up cards that are in your right hand on top of the face-up cards that are in your left hand. Turn the deck over. The chosen card is now on top.

◆ *Key-Card Control* ◆

In some instances, using a key card for control works best. For example, you might want to bring the chosen card to within a fairly high number of cards from the top. This control would do perfectly, as I'll explain.

Before the spectator chooses a card, sneak a peek at the bottom card of the deck. This is your key card. You can do this as you separate the deck in two, preparing to do a riffle shuffle. Easier yet, look at the bottom card as you tap the side of the deck on the table, apparently evening up the cards. Then, when you shuffle, keep the card on the bottom.

So you know the bottom card of the deck. Fan out the deck, and a spectator selects a card. Close up the deck. From the top of the deck, lift off a small packet of cards and drop it onto the table. Lift off another small packet and drop it on top of the first one. After dropping several packets like this, say to the spectator, "Put your card here whenever you want." After you drop one of your packets, he places his card on top. You put the rest of the deck on top of it. Even up the cards and pick them up. The key card which you peeked at is now above the chosen card.

Start fanning through the cards, faces towards yourself. Mutter something such as, "This is going to be really hard." Fan off several cards. Cut them to the rear of the deck. Fan off several more. Again, cut them to the rear. You're establishing a pattern so that it won't seem so odd when you finally cut the chosen card into position.

Let's say you simply want the card available on top of the deck. Continue fanning groups of cards and placing them at the rear until you see that you'll soon arrive at the key card. Cut the cards so that the key card becomes the top card of the deck. Just below it, of course, is the chosen card. Turn the deck face down.

"I can't seem to find your card." Turn over the top card of the deck (the key card). "This isn't it, is it?" No. Turn the card over and stick it into the middle of the deck. Turn the deck face up. "How about this one?" No. Take the bottom card and stick it into the middle of the deck. Turn the deck face down. The chosen card is at your disposal on top of the deck.

Suppose, for purposes of a specific trick, you want the chosen card to be 10th from the top. Again you start by fanning off small groups and cutting them to the rear of the deck. When you get to the chosen card, you start counting to yourself. You count the chosen card as "One." Count the next card as "Two." Cut the cards so that the card at "Ten" becomes the top card. The chosen card is now 10th from the top.

Clearly, you can use the same method to arrange to spell the chosen card from the top, dealing off one card for each letter in the spelling.

FALSE CUTS

♣ ♦ ♥ ♠

♦ *All in the Hands* ♦

Nelson Lyford developed a deceptively simple false cut which is done entirely in the hands. It must be performed casually. Don't call attention to it. At the appropriate time, just *do* it.

Place the deck well back on the palm of the left hand (Illus. 3). Cut off the top half with your right hand and place it on your hand to the right of the other half (Illus. 4).

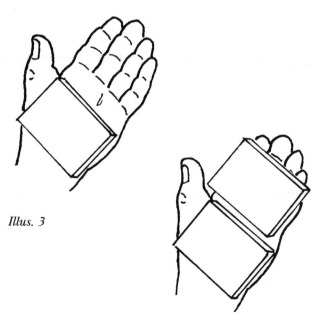

Illus. 3

Illus. 4

Lift off the bottom half with your right hand. With your left hand, slide the other half on top of the cards in your right hand. The deck is back in its original order.

◆ *Roll-Up Cut* ◆

I designed this cut specifically for the gambling trick *Really Wild* (see page 93). No sleight is involved, and it keeps the entire deck in order. There's no reason why it can't be used in other tricks to retain a group of cards or a single card on the top or bottom of the deck.

The cut certainly does not look ordinary. If you use it, I recommend that you give it a fancy name to go with its fancy appearance. For instance, you might say, "I'll just give the cards the *super-duper roll-up cut*," or, "To make sure the cards are mixed, I'll do the *up-and-down-lay-'em-out-and-pick-'em-up cut*."

You start with the deck face down in the dealing position in your left hand. Flip the deck face up with your left thumb. With your right thumb, lift about a quarter of the deck from the left side. Pivot this packet in an arc to the right, as though opening a book from the back (refer to Illus. 2). Let the packet fall face down onto your right hand. Place the face-down packet down to your left.

Flip the rest of the deck over with your left thumb so that the cards are now face down. This time, with your right thumb, pivot about a third of the deck from the left side. Let this packet fall face up onto your right hand. Set the packet down an inch or two to the right of the first packet.

Again, flip the rest of the deck over with your left thumb; the cards are now face up. With your right thumb, turn over about half of the cards and set them face up on the table to the right of the other two packets.

Remaining in your left hand is a packet of face-up cards. Set the packet down face up to the right of the others. Pause, saying, "Now comes the hard part."

With your right hand, grasp the right side of the packet. Turn this packet over on top of the packet to its left, as though closing the back portion of a book (Illus. 5). In the same way, turn the combined packet over and place it on the packet to its left. Once more, turn the combined packet over and place it on the packet to its left—the first packet you placed down.

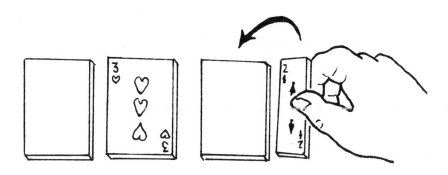

Illus. 5

Even up the cards. The deck is face down and in the precise order it was at the beginning.

The first time you follow this description with a deck of cards, it may seem that the cards can't possibly be in their original order. It just doesn't seem logical. Maybe I should have called it "the illogical cut."

Note: When lifting off the packets to place them onto the table, you may prefer to grasp them at the ends with the palm-down right hand, fingers at the outer end and thumb at the inner end. As with the other method, you pivot the packet in an arc to the right, as though opening a book from the back. Then place the packet onto the table.

FORCES

◆ *One-Cut Force* ◆

For this force, you must know the top card of the deck. An easy way is to peek at the bottom card. Then give the deck an overhand shuffle, shuffling off the last few cards singly so that the bottom card ends up on top.

Hold the deck face down in your left hand. Extend the deck towards a spectator, saying, "Please cut off about half, turn the cut-off group face up, and place it face up on the deck."

**Point to the first
face-down card.**

Illus. 6

After the spectator does this, turn your left hand palm down and put the deck on the table. Spread all the cards out. Point to the first face-down card after the face-up cards (Illus. 6). Say to the spectator, "Take a look at your card, please."

It is, of course, the original top card.

◆ *Crisscross Force* ◆

Again, you must know the top card of the deck. Set the deck on the table. Ask a spectator to cut off a pile and place it on the table. Pick up the bottom portion and place it crosswise on the cut-off portion.

Chat with the spectator for a moment so that he has a chance to forget about the true position of the two piles. (This is known as "time misdirection.") Point to the top card of the lower pile, saying, "Take a look at your card, please." As before, it's the original top card of the deck.

GLIDE

♣ ♦ ♥ ♠

This is a method of secretly exchanging one card for another. You show the bottom card and apparently place it on the table. Only it is not the same card; you actually deal out the second card from the bottom.

Hold the deck in the left hand at the sides from above, letting a little more than the first joint of the middle fingers extend below the deck. Lift the deck to a vertical position, showing the bottom card. Lower the deck to a horizontal position.

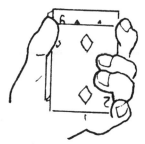

Illus. 7

With the middle fingers of the left hand, draw the bottom card back about half an inch (Illus. 7). With the tips of the right fingers, draw out the second card from the bottom. As the card comes forward about an inch, your right thumb grips it on top. The card is pulled completely out and set face down on the table.

At the exact instant that the card hits the table, push the bottom card back to its original position with the left little finger.

20

Tricks

DISCOVERY

Discovery is the theme of some of the most imaginative card tricks, yet the basic idea is one of the simplest. A card is chosen, and the magician locates it.

◆ *No Touch, No Feel* ◆

Long, long ago, magician George Sands came up with this superb, puzzling trick. I have added a few wrinkles.

Since Ginny is quite bright, ask her to assist you. Hand her the deck of cards, saying, "Throughout this experiment, Ginny, I'm not going to touch the cards. To start with, I'd like you to give the deck a good shuffle." When she finishes, say, "Now I'd like you to deal the cards into a pile." Make sure you *don't* say, "Count the cards into a pile." At this point, you don't want her thinking about numbers. You, however, are counting the cards to yourself—as casually as you can. When she has dealt ten cards, say, "You can stop whenever you wish."

Continue to count the cards silently until she stops dealing. Turn away, saying, "Please set the rest of the deck aside. Now I'd like you to think of a number . . . say, less than 10. Remember that number. Next, look at the card that lies at that number from the top of your pile. For instance, if you thought of the number 5, you'd look at the card that lies 5th from the top of your pile. Please remember that card and leave it at that number."

When she's ready, continue, "Ginny, set your packet down and pick up the rest of the deck. Remember that number you thought of? Please deal that same number of cards from the deck on top of your pile. So, if you thought of the number 5, you'd deal five cards from the deck onto your pile. Then set the deck down again and pick up your pile.

"The first person to try this experiment was an Australian, so we must honor him by doing a 'down-under' shuffle. Deal the top card of your pile onto the table. Now put the next card underneath your pile. Deal the next card onto the table and place the next card underneath your pile. Continue like this until all your cards are on the table."

When she's done, say, "Pick up your entire pile and place it on top of the deck. Even up all the cards."

Turn back to the group. "Ginny, at no time have I touched the cards, and I'm not going to touch them now. Neither you nor I know exactly where your card is in the deck. Still, there is a certain aura which is attached to the card you've chosen, and I'm going to try to detect that aura. Please deal the cards slowly into a pile."

Ginny deals the cards down. "Slow down," you say, as she nears the selected card. "I feel that it's very close." Finally, you say, "Stop! What's the name of the card you thought of." She names it; you point to the last card she dealt onto the pile. She turns it over and, of course, it's that very card.

You should be ashamed of yourself, bamboozling Ginny with a trick that's as easy to do as this one. As I mentioned, before you turn away, you note the number of cards that are dealt. With a very easy calculation, this number tells you at what number from the top the assistant's card will be when she slowly deals the cards out.

You divide by 2 the number of cards dealt out. If you end up with a number followed by ½, you take the next whole number. This is the number at which the card will lie near the end of the trick. But if you divide by 2 and end up with a whole number, you divide *that* number by 2. And you continue to divide by 2 until you do get a number that ends in ½. When you finally get ½ at the end, take the next whole number.

For instance, suppose the assistant deals out 15 cards. Divide 15 by 2, getting 7½. Take the next whole number, 8. When the assistant deals out the cards at the end, the selected card will be 8th from the top.

Suppose the assistant dealt 14 cards at the beginning. Divide this by 2, getting 7. But you must get a number with ½ at the end, so divide the 7 by 2. This gives you 3½. Take the next whole number, which is 4. The chosen card will end up 4th from the top.

Let's take an extreme example. The assistant deals out 24 cards at the beginning. You divide this by 2, getting 12. You divide the 12 by 2, getting 6. You divide the 6 by 2, getting 3. You divide the 3 by 2, getting 1½. At last, a number with ½ at the end! Take the next whole number greater than 1½, which is 2. At the end, the assistant's card will be 2nd from the top.

♦ *Sheer Luck* ♦

This is my version of a trick of unknown origin. In some respects, it is similar to *No Touch, No Feel,* but the overall effect and the climax are quite different.

The trick works best when you display a sense of curiosity and wonderment throughout. You and the audience are participating in an experiment; heaven only knows what will happen!

"I'd like to experiment with something I've never tried before," you explain, smiling engagingly to prove that you're not lying through your teeth. "Mel, would you please help out."

Hand him the deck, asking him to shuffle the cards. "Now what? Oh, I have an idea. Why don't you cut off a good-sized bunch of cards and shuffle them up? I'll turn my back while you're doing it."

Turn away. Continue: "Let's see ... maybe you should look at the top card of that bunch. Yeah, that's a good idea. In fact, show that card around and then put it back on top of the bunch.

"Hey, I've got an inspiration! Mel, set that bunch down and pick up the rest of the deck. Now we all know that 7 is a lucky number, so think of a number from 1 to 7. Got one? Then deal that many cards from the deck onto your pile ... right on top of your card." As he does this, you might mutter something like, "This is really getting good."

Continue: "Okay, Mel. Set down the rest of the deck and pick up the pile containing your card. Put that pile right on top of the rest of the deck and even up the cards." Turn back to the group and pick up the deck. "All I have to do is find your card. Now we're getting to the part that I haven't quite worked out yet." Casually fan off eight cards from the top of the group. (Don't count these aloud; you make it appear that any small number will do.) Hold this packet of eight cards and set the rest of the deck aside. "Maybe it'll work better if we have fewer cards." Riffle the group of eight next to your ear. "Sounds like your card's here, all right."

Have Mel pick up the rest of the deck. Set the packet of eight on the table. "You know what might help, Mel? Remember that number you dealt on top of your card? I'll turn away again, and you deal that same number on top of the pile again." Point to the pile of eight cards so that he'll know exactly what to do. Turn away while he does his dealing. Turn back and have Mel set the deck aside and pick up the pile containing his card.

"It's pretty obvious what we have to try now, Mel. We have to eliminate lots of cards. Please put the top card on the bottom. Then deal the next card onto the table. Next, put the top card on the bottom. And again deal the next card onto the table." Have him continue this deal until only one card remains in his hands.

"What was your card, Mel?" He names it. It's the one he's holding.

Note: The deal used at the end of this trick is the opposite of the "Australian shuffle." In the latter, the *down-under* deal, a card is dealt onto the table and then one placed on the bottom, and so on. This is an *under-down* deal. The first card goes on the bottom, the next on the table, and so on.

♦ *Double Discovery* ♦

Whoever discovered the clever principle used here should be very proud, for it has been incorporated into any number of excellent tricks. This is my favorite.

You'll need a complete 52-card deck and two willing assistants—Wendy and Grant, for instance.

Hand Wendy the deck. "We're going to have both you and Grant choose a card, Wendy. But we want to be absolutely fair. So each of you should have exactly half the deck. Would you please count off 26 cards and give them to Grant."

After she does so, turn your back. Give the following instructions, with appropriate pauses: "I'd like each of you to shuffle your cards. Look at the bottom card of your group and notice its value. Now very quietly deal off that many cards from the top of your group. Just deal them into a pile on the table. If the bottom card is a 6, for example, you'd deal off 6 cards from the top of your group. A jack counts as 11, a queen as 12, and a king as 13.

"Once you've dealt off the cards, you don't need to remember the number. Just look at the top card of the pile you dealt off. Please remember it; that's your chosen card.

"Wendy, you're holding a group of cards. Please place this group on top of the cards that Grant dealt off.

"Grant, place the cards that you're holding on top of the pile that Wendy dealt off.

"One more job, Wendy, and then we're done. Put either pile on top of the other, and even the cards up."

When she finishes, turn back to the group. "It's pretty obvious that no ordinary human being could locate the two selected cards. But I am no ordinary human being. As a matter of fact, I'm from Krypton . . . or is it Mars? I can never remember."

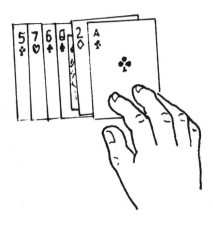

Illus. 8

Pick up the deck and hold it face down. You will deal the entire deck into a face-up pile, spreading the cards from left to right as you deal them (Illus. 8). Deal out 12 cards face up. As you place the 13th card face up onto the pile, think to yourself, "King." As you deal the next card onto the pile, think, "Queen." As you deal the next, think, "Jack." Continue all the way down to ace. As you do this, at some point the card you're dealing will match the card you're thinking. For instance, you might think to yourself, "Six," and the card you're placing onto the pile is a six. Don't stop or pause at this point, but continue on as though nothing had happened. The fact is, however, that six tells you everything you need to know about the two chosen cards. The card following it is one of the chosen cards. Furthermore, the six tells you that the other chosen card is 6th from the bottom of the deck.

So you have dealt a 6, and it matches the number you were thinking. Deal the next card (one of the selected cards) slightly out of line to mark the position of the 6. This is important, as I will explain later.

You now continue dealing the rest of the deck face up. Spread out the cards. As you do this, mentally count backwards from the face of the deck to the 6th card from the bottom. Pass one of your hands back and forth over the cards. Let your hand fall on the first chosen card that you noticed, the one that followed the six. Push this card forward. "I believe that this is one of the chosen cards. Whose is it?"

Let's say that Grant admits that it's his. "Good. Now I must find Wendy's card." Again pass your hand over the cards. This time, let it fall onto the 6th card from the bottom. Push this card forward. "And this must be your card, Wendy."

Another Example: You deal 12 cards one at a time into a face-up pile. When you deal out the 13th card face up, you think to yourself, "King." You continue the sequence, mentally counting one card lower each time you deal a card. Suppose that you're thinking, "Nine," and you deal out a nine at the same time. This means that the next card you deal will be one of the chosen cards, and that the other chosen card will be 9th from the bottom of the deck.

Sometimes, as you go through the backward sequence from king to ace, more than one card will match up. Suppose, for instance, that you mentally match both jack and 3. The card after the jack might be one of the chosen cards, but so might the card after the 3. What do you do?

After you come to each match, you move the next card a bit out of line. This eliminates the possibility of any later confusion. After you finish dealing out the entire deck, you can easily go back and look at the two possibilities. So a jack matched, and suppose that right after it came the seven of clubs. And a 3 matched, and let's say that right after it came the ace of diamonds. You'll have to eliminate one of the possibilities. The best way is the most direct way. Simply say, "Did one of you choose an ace?" If the answer is no, say, "I didn't think so." You now know that one of the chosen cards is the seven of clubs (the one that followed the jack), and that the other chosen card is 11th from the bottom.

If one of your assistants *did* choose an ace, you say, "I thought so." Push the ace of diamonds forward. "I think it's this one." The matching card just before the ace was a 3, so you now know that the other chosen card is 3rd from the bottom.

♦ *Four Times Four* ♦

Years ago, I read a trick in a magic magazine in which four spectators each think of a card, and the magician discovers all the chosen cards. Unfortunately, I couldn't figure out the explanation. Either something was wrong with the write-up, or I was extremely dense. Since I preferred the former theory and I very much liked the plot, I worked out my own method.

Ask a spectator to shuffle the deck, take four cards for himself, and distribute four cards to each of three other spectators. The rest of the deck is set aside.

Tell the four spectators, "Please look through your cards and figure out one card that you like. Remember that card. Then mix up your four cards so that even you don't know which one is your card."

Mentally number the spectators from left to right as 1, 2, 3, and 4. Take Spectator 4's packet. Place Spectator 3's packet on top of it. Spectator 2's packet goes on top of the combined packets. And Spectator 1's packet goes on top of all.

"If you don't mind, I'll mix the cards a bit. In fact, I'll give them the famous *holy-moley-what-the-heck-kind-of-a-shuffle-is-that? shuffle.*"

Take the top card into your right hand, just as though you were going to deal it. Take the next card on top of that card, grasping it with your right thumb. Push off the next card with your left thumb. Grasp it with the right fingers, taking it below the two in your right hand. The next card goes on top of those in your right hand. Continue alternating like this until all the cards are in your right hand. "Let's try that again."

Perform the same peculiar shuffle. "That should do it."

With your right hand, take off the top four cards of the packet, dealing them *one on top of the other,* so that their order is reversed. Set the rest of the packet down. Fan out the four cards so that the four spectators can see the faces. "Does anyone see his card here?"

Whatever the answers, close up the cards and deal them out from left to right—in a special way. From your left to right, consider that there are positions 1, 2, 3, and 4 on the table—matching the positions of the four spectators. When any spectator sees his card displayed, that card is dealt face down at the appropriate position; the others are dealt face up. Suppose that, on your first display, Spectators 1 and 4 have seen their cards. Deal the top card (signifying Spectator 1) face down at Position 1. Deal the second card (signifying Spectator 2) face up at Position 2. Deal the third card (signifying Spectator 3) face up at Position 3. Deal the fourth card (signifying Spectator 4) face down at Position 4.

Since Spectators 1 and 4 saw their cards, you dealt the first and fourth cards face down at Positions 1 and 4; the others were dealt face up (Illus. 9).

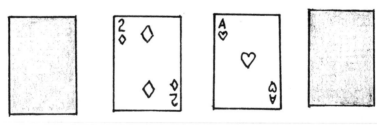

Illus. 9

Pick up the packet, which now contains 12 cards. Fan out the top four cards of the packet. Take them from the packet, *retaining their order.* Set the rest of the packet down. Hold the four cards so that the four spectators can see them. Again ask if anyone sees his card. Let's suppose that Spectator 3 sees his card. Deal the first two cards face up on top of the cards at Positions 1 and 2, respectively. Deal the third card face down on top of the card at Position 3. The fourth card is dealt face up on top of the card at Position 4. In other words, since Spectator 3 saw his card, it is dealt face down; the others are dealt face up (Illus. 10).

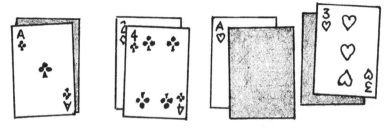

Illus. 10

Pick up the packet, which now contains eight cards. With the right hand, take off the top four cards, *one on top of the other,* reversing their order. Set the remainder of the packet down. Show the four cards you counted off, as before. If a spectator should see his card, that card would be dealt face down at the appropriate number; the others would be dealt out face up on their respective piles. But no one sees his card, so all four are dealt face up on the appropriate piles.

Pick up the remaining four cards and fan them out, show- ing them. In this instance, you know that Spectator 2 will see his card. So, as you go ahead and deal the cards onto their piles from left to right, you deal the second card face down on the pile at Position 2. The others are dealt face up.

With your right hand, pick up the face-up cards at Position 1 and place them, still face up, into your left hand. Pick up the face-down card at Position 1. Ask Spectator 1 for the name of his chosen card. When he names it, turn the card over and hand it to him.

Do the same for the remaining three spectators, working from left to right. You have managed to identify all four chosen cards.

Note: You show a group of four cards four times. The first and third times, you take the cards one on top of the other, reversing their order. The second and fourth times, you fan out four from the top and take them in the right hand, retaining their order.

♦ *Sixes and Nines* ♦

Are you ready for a trick that has fooled some of the most knowledgeable card experts in the world? This is it. And Wally Wilson is the performer. He says that the basic trick is very old. But I was not familiar with it. Of course Wally has added a few wrinkles, along with his own special performance magic.

Preparation: Take the sixes and the nines from the deck. Place the sixes on top and the nines on the bottom.

Start by giving the deck a casual riffle shuffle. Let's assume you have the bottom half in your left hand and the top half in your right hand. Riffle off at least a half dozen cards with your left hand before you start meshing in the cards. This pretty much guarantees that a half dozen or so cards from your right hand will fall on top. It also guarantees that the sixes will still be on top and the nines on the bottom.

Lana will be delighted to assist you. Hand her the deck and say, "Lana, I'd like you to deal out the entire deck into four piles, going from left to right. Just deal them as though you were dealing out four hands in a card game—only neater."

When she finishes, continue: "Please pick up any one of the piles. Fan through the cards and take out any one you want. Put it aside for a minute while you set the pile back down. Now look at your card and show it around, but don't let me see its face."

After everyone but you has had a chance to see the card, go on: "Lana, put the card on top of any one of the piles." She does so. "Now if you want to, you can cut that pile. Or, if you prefer, place one of the other piles on top of it." If she cuts the pile on which her card sits, have her then stack all four piles in any order she wishes. If she does not cut that pile, have her proceed directly to the stacking of the piles.

The deck is now given at least two complete cuts. "You're the one who's been handling the deck, Lana, so it's certain that I have no idea of where your card is." Spread the deck face up onto the table so that all the cards can be seen. "Nevertheless, some people suspect that I sneak cards out of the deck. I want you to notice that your card is still there. I'll look away while you check it out." As you say this, spread through the cards as though further separating them to provide a better view. Actually, you're looking for the sixes and nines. In one instance, you will find a 6 and a 9 separated by one card. That card is the one chosen by the spectator; remember it.

Mostly you'll find a 6 and a 9 side by side. If Lana cut the packet before stacking the cards, you'll find a lone 6 and a lone 9 somewhere. Just keep in mind that you're looking for the card that separates a 6 and a 9.

After you note this card, which will take just a few seconds, avert your head. "When you're done, Lana, gather up the cards, please, and then give them a good shuffle."

At this point, you can take the deck from Lana and reveal the card any way you wish. You could read her mind, for instance. Wally Wilson prefers this startling conclusion that includes an easy sleight I'd never seen before:

Fan through the cards, faces towards yourself. Cut some to the top. Fan through more cards and cut another small group to the top. Eventually, cut the cards so that the chosen card becomes the third card from the top. As you do all this, mutter things like, "It has to be here somewhere. I don't know. I *should* be able to figure this out." After the last cut, turn the deck face down. "I think I have it, Lana. But this is very difficult, so I want four guesses. I probably won't need all four guesses, but you never know . . ."

The deck is in your left hand in the dealing position. Lift your left hand so that the bottom card faces the group (Illus.

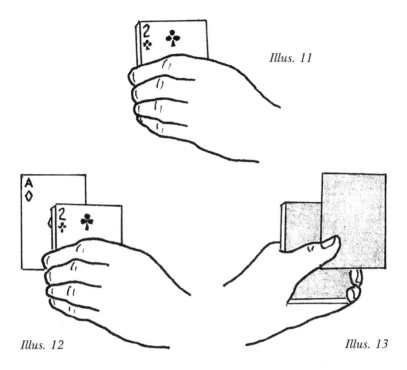

Illus. 11

Illus. 12

Illus. 13

11). With your right thumb, pull up the top card diagonally. Move your right hand away so that about half the card is displayed (Illus. 12). The left thumb holds the bottom left corner of the card (Illus. 13). "Here's my first guess. Is this your card, Lana?" No, it isn't.

With the right hand, push the card back so that it is even with the others. At this point, you're still holding the cards in a vertical position. Lower the left hand to the regular dealing position. Deal the top card face down onto the table to your right.

Again raise the deck to a vertical position. Show the next card in the same way as before. Wrong again! Push the card back, turn the deck to a horizontal position, and deal the top card onto the table to the left of the first card.

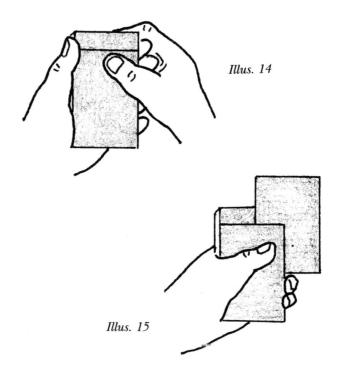

Illus. 14

Illus. 15

Once more raise the deck to a vertical position. This time, you'll perform a deceptive move that I call the *thumb glide.* Move the right hand up to the deck, as though to display the next card. As you chat with the spectators about your hopes for your third guess, move the top card down about half an inch with your right thumb. This is easily accomplished by using *very light* pressure (Illus. 14). Then pull up the *second card from the top* and display it as you did the others (Illus. 15). You're wrong again, of course. Push the card back with the right fingers and push the actual top card back into position with the right thumb. *Now* lower the deck and deal the top card onto the table to the left of the other two cards. You have cleverly and successfully managed to switch the card you showed for the chosen card.

You want to show a fourth card, but the spectators just saw the present top card. So you say, "Lana, this doesn't seem to be working. Maybe I'll have better luck if you cut the cards." Place the deck on the table and let her cut it. Pick the deck up and show a fourth card in the same way as you did the first two. Failure! Give Lana a look of mock disgust, saying, "Thanks a lot, Lana." The fourth card goes face down to the left of the others.

Place your right hand on the two cards on the right, and your left hand on the two cards to the left. Say, "Left or right, Lana?" Whatever she replies, lift your left hand. Pull the two cards beneath your right hand towards you. Turn one of them over. "So you say that this is not your card, Lana." Right. Turn the other card over. "And this isn't your card." Again, right.

"Hand me one of these cards, please." Indicate the two face-down cards on the table. If she hands you the card on your left, turn it over, saying, "And this isn't your card."

If she hands you the card on your right, take it, and set it in front of her. Turn over the other face-down card, saying, "And this isn't your card."

In either instance, the chosen card remains face down on the table. "So, what is your card, Lana?" She names it. Make a few magical gestures over the chosen card and then ask Lana to turn it over. At last you've located the chosen card.

Spelling

♦ *The Impossible Nine* ♦

As far as I know, Jim Steinmeyer discovered the principle used in this trick. This is basically the same as what he calls the *Nine Card Problem,* with a few of my own ideas thrown in.

There are not many card tricks in which the spectator handles the deck throughout. And, of these, very few are really effective. The two discovery tricks, *No Touch, No Feel* (page 22) and *Sheer Luck* (page 25), and the four-aces trick, *It's Out of My Hands* (page 53), are among my favorites, but this one is certainly one of the very best.

Ask Mary Lou to help out. "I don't know if you know this, but the number nine has peculiar qualities, not only in mathematics, but also in magic. So I would like you to shuffle the deck and then count off nine cards." She does so. "Shuffle those up and then look at the bottom card. This is your chosen card, so make sure you remember it. Now let's mix things up a bit. Place the top card on the bottom of your pile, and deal the next card on the table. Deal the next card under the pile, and the next one on the table." Have her continue to do this until all the cards are in a pile on the table. Ask Mary Lou to pick up the pile.

Turn your back, saying, "There is no way in the world that I can tell what or where your card is. Please think of the value of your card. For example, if you chose the five of spades, you would think of five. Now spell out the value of your card, dealing one card into a pile for each letter in the spelling.

With *five,* you would deal one card on the table for F. Deal another on top of it for I. Deal another on top of that for V. And deal another card on the pile for E. Do this very quietly."

When she finishes say, "You have some cards left in your hand. Place these on top of the cards you dealt on the table. Pick up the entire pile. Now please spell out the word *of,* placing one card in a pile for each letter. In other words, deal two cards into a pile. Then place the rest of the cards on top of these, and pick up the entire pile."

When Mary Lou is done, continue, "In the same way, spell out your suit into a pile . . . either clubs, hearts, spades, or diamonds. If the suit were clubs, you would spell out C-L-U-B-S. Then place the rest of the cards on top of the pile and pick up the entire pile."

When Mary Lou is done, turn back to the group. "I think you'll agree that there's no way I could know the position of your card, nor the name of your card. After all, you could have spelled two, T-W-O, or three, T-H-R-E-E. Or any of the other values. And there's a big difference between the spelling of clubs, C-L-U-B-S, and diamonds, D-I-A-M-O-N-D-S. So how will we find your card? We'll have to resort to magic, or—as I like to refer to it—luck. I'll let you pick out something to spell. Mary Lou, do you believe in sorcery, mysticism?" If she says yes, say, "In other words, you believe in magic, right?" She does. So have her spell the word *magic,* dealing one card into a pile for each letter in the spelling. Ask her to name her card. Then have her turn over the last card she dealt.

But what if she answers no, when you ask, "Mary Lou, do you believe in sorcery, mysticism?" You continue, "In other words, you think this is just a trick." Have her spell the word *trick,* as just described for the word *magic.* Since each word consists of five letters, the last card she deals will always be the chosen one.

How in the world does this thing work? The *under-down* deal brings the chosen card to third from the top. Using a nine-card pile, when you spell the complete name of any card, as described, the 3rd card from the top will become the 5th card from the top.

You can reveal it any way you wish. The way I wish is to pretend to offer them a choice of words.

Note: In the final phase of the trick, it's important that you ask, "Do you believe in sorcery, mysticism?" When she answers yes, it's perfectly natural that you should have her spell the word *magic*. If she answers no, you have her spell the word *trick*. And you have left her with the impression that she could have spelled out *sorcery* or *mysticism*. This is a small point, to be sure, but such touches are what turn a good trick into a miracle.

◆ *Yes or No* ◆

Werner Miller is the inventor of this simple, fast, effective spelling trick. I handle the beginning of the trick a bit differently.

Ask Harlan to help you out. Perform the *One-Cut Force* (page 18). Have Harlan shuffle the deck and return it to you. You, of course, know the name of his card.

"Harlan, I'm going to go through the deck and pick out nine cards. If I'm lucky, one of them will be the one you picked. The odds are against it, but I'm going to hope for the best."

Fan through the cards, faces towards yourself. Pick out any eight cards, placing them in a face-down pile on the table. The last card you take from the deck is the chosen card. This is placed on top of the pile. Set the rest aside.

Tap the pile. "I'm pretty sure I have your card here, Harlan. Now I'm going to wish for even more luck. I'll ask you a question. You can answer yes or no. If you answer yes, I'll spell out *yes*, placing one card on the bottom for each letter in the spelling. The next card I'll put on the table. Then I'll spell out *yes* again in exactly the same way. Eventually, I'll have one card left. Who knows—maybe it'll be yours. If you answer no to the question, I'll spell out *no*. Again, I'll put one card on the bottom for each letter and place the next card on the table. And I'll keep doing that until I have one card left. Ready for your question?"

He is.

You can have some fun by asking him one of those "can't-win" questions, like, "Do you still cheat at cards?" or, "Have you stopped stealing from the collection plate?" But neither the question nor the answer actually matters to the success of the trick. Simply spell out *yes* or *no,* as described above. The last card you're holding will be the one he chose.

SETUP

♣ ♦ ♥ ♠

These tricks, in one way or another, require some preparation. In some instances, only a card or two must be placed in position. In others, a number of cards must be set up in advance. I believe that a really good trick is worth the bit of extra trouble.

♦ *Blind Chance* ♦

I have seen versions of this principle used by both Nick Trost and Ed Marlo, so it's hard to know whom to credit. Regardless, it's a wondrous trick. My variation differs somewhat in order to create what I think is a stronger climax.

You may make the necessary preparation ahead of time, but I find it just as easy to do this: Turn away from the group, saying, "Excuse me for just a moment. I have to pick out a proper prediction card, and this requires extreme concentration." Turn over any card about 6th from the bottom of the deck. Find its mate—the card that matches it in color and value. Remove this from the deck. Turn back to the group, the deck face down in one hand and your prediction card face down in the other.

Let's say that you have turned the ten of spades face up so that it's several cards from the bottom of the deck. Your prediction card, then, is the ten of clubs. Place this face down on the table, saying, "Here's my prediction. But its accuracy will depend on someone else." Single out Dorothy. "Will you help me, Dorothy? If we're on the same wavelength, this should work perfectly."

Hand her the deck. "Please place the cards behind your back. I want you to be able to choose a card without being influenced by me or anyone else in any way at all."

Make sure that Dorothy stands so that no one can see the cards.

"Reach into the middle of the deck, Dorothy, and take out any card. Turn it face up and set it on top of the deck. Now give the cards a cut and even them up."

When she is done, have her hand you the deck.

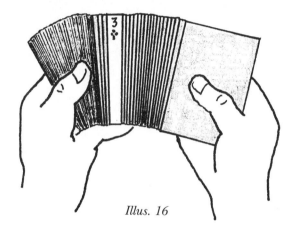

Illus. 16

Fan through the cards so that all can see. When you come to a face-up card, fan a few cards beyond (Illus. 16). Next, fan back so that the face-up card is on top of the face-down cards in your left hand. Separate your hands; the face-up card remains on top of those in your left hand, while the balance of the deck is in your right hand. Place all the cards that are in your right hand *below* those in your left hand. You are now holding a face-down deck with a face-up card on top. "So your card is . . ." Name it. Naturally, it's the card that *you* previously turned face up. Place the card face up next to your prediction card.

Turn the deck face up. Murmur, "Let's see if you accidentally turned over more than one card." Casually fan through about four-fifths of the deck, showing the faces. "No, I guess not." Close up the deck and set it aside.

"Dorothy, we'll now find out whether we're on the same wavelength. If we are, these two cards should match each other in color and value." Turn over your prediction card, showing that it matches her choice.

Note: At the end of the trick, you have a face-up card near the top of the deck. You have several options. You could make this your last trick, and simply put the cards away. Or you could do a few tricks where the face-up card will not show up. Then, at a break in the action, step aside and turn the card over. My favorite is to do a "take-a-card" trick. Turn away while the assistant shows the card around. Naturally, while your back is turned, you turn the face-up card over.

♦ *The Ideal Card Trick* ♦

Here's the ideal card trick: A card is selected, you do something miraculous with it, and no skill is required. Here we have the invention of U.F. Grant, a creative giant in the field of magic.

Preparation: Place any 4 face up fourth from the bottom of the deck.

Daphne may have a funny name, but she sure is a good sport, so fan the cards out and ask her to select a card. Make sure, of course, that you do not spread the cards out near the bottom; no need to disclose the face-up 4. Have her show the card around and then replace it on top of the deck. Give the deck a complete cut and set it on the table.

"Daphne, I am going to attempt a feat that is nearly impossible. I am going to try to turn a card face up in the middle of the deck. Will it be your card? Oh, no, that would be too easy. Instead, I will try to turn over a card that will tell us where your card is. I can't believe how tough this is going to be."

Pick up the deck and give it a little riffle at the ends. "I hope that works." Fan through the cards until you come to the face-up 4. "Ah, here we have a face-up card, a 4." Set the cards above the 4 onto the table. Lift off the 4 and place it, still face up, on the table. "So let's count off four cards." Deal off four cards, counting aloud. Place your finger on the last card dealt off. "What was the name of your card, Daphne?" She names it, and you turn it over.

◆ *Seven for Luck* ◆

Len Searles created this superb trick. Here's my variation.

Preparation: Place a 7 on top, followed by seven face-up cards.

Address Richard: "I'd like you to select a card completely by chance, so we should follow a certain procedure." Extend the deck towards him on the palm of your hand. "Richard, please cut off a substantial group of cards, turn the group face up, and set it back onto the deck."

When he finishes, even up the cards, and hand him the deck. "Now just fan down to the card you cut to and take a look at it . . . I'll look away." Avert your head while he looks at his card. "Done? Okay, then turn those face-up cards face down again and put them back on top of the deck, right on top of your chosen card."

Take the deck from Richard and show that the cards are all evened up. Take off the top card with your right hand, but don't let anyone see it. Glance at it. It doesn't matter what the card is because you're going to miscall it anyway. Put the deck behind your back with the left hand and the card with your right hand, saying, "Okay, I'm going to stick this 7 face up into the middle of the deck and hope for the best." Actually, you simply place it back on top of the deck and bring the cards forward.

"Seven! That's definitely good luck. Let's see where the 7 is, and then we'll count from there." Turn the deck face up and fan through until you come to the face-down card, which, of course, is a 7. Take the cards you fanned off and set them aside. Pick off the 7 and turn it over so that all can see. "There's the 7," you declare, for those who are far-sighted. Set the 7 aside. "So we'll count off seven cards. Richard, what was your card?" He names it. You count off seven cards and there it is . . . on the 7th card.

♦ *What Do You Think?* ♦

A spectator merely *thinks* of a card and, in practically no time, you—with your incredible magical powers—locate it.

Preparation: First, unknown to all, put all the eights and nines on the bottom of the deck. The order of these placed cards doesn't matter.

Ready? Say to Greta, "I'd like you to think of a number *between* 1 and 10." (Be sure to say "between," because you don't want her to choose 1 or 10.) "Now I'll show you ten cards one at a time. Please remember the card that lies at the number you thought of."

Avert your head as you hold up the top card, face towards Greta. At the same time, say, "One." Take the next card in front of the first and show it to Greta, saying, "Two." Continue through the 10th card. Replace the 10 cards on top of the deck. They are, of course, in the same order.

"Greta, I'm going to put these cards behind my back and perform an astonishing feat. I'm going to put your chosen card in a position where you yourself will locate it with a randomly chosen card."

Put the deck behind your back. Take off the top card and put it on the bottom. Turn the deck face up. To yourself, *very quietly* count off the nine bottom cards, one on top of the other. Place this packet on top of the deck. Turn the deck face down and bring it forward. You now have an indifferent card on top, followed by the 8s and 9s.

"Okay, Greta, everything is ready. All I need to know is the number you thought of." She names the number. Let's say the number is 6. Count aloud as you deal five cards onto the table. When you say "six" aloud, lift off the 6th card, turn it over, and continue to hold it. It will be either an 8 or a 9. Whichever it is, announce its value, and say, "Let's hope that this card will help us find your card."

If the card is an 8, place it face up onto the pile you dealt off. In another pile, deal eight cards, counting aloud. Ask Greta to name her card. Turn over the last card dealt. It is the one she thought of.

If the last card you lift off is a 9, call attention to it, and then turn it face down on top of the deck. Deal off nine cards, counting aloud. As before, the last card will be the one chosen.

Summary: When the spectator gives the number she thought of, you deal off one less than this number, counting aloud. When you name the last number of the count, you hang on to the card. Turn it over, still holding it. If it's an 8, drop it on top of the pile you just dealt; deal off eight cards from the rest of the deck and turn over the last card. If it's a 9, replace it face down on top of the deck; deal off nine cards from the deck and turn over the last card.

♦ *A Face-Up Miracle* ♦

Doug Maihafer developed an astonishing trick which would ordinarily require considerable skill at sleight of hand. His trick, however, requires only a bit of preparation.

Ahead of time, note the bottom card of a blue-backed deck of cards. Go through a red-backed deck and find the duplicate to this card. Place the red-backed duplicate *face up* second from the bottom.

So the situation might be this: You have a blue-backed deck. The bottom card is the blue-backed jack of hearts. The second card from the bottom is a red-backed jack of hearts, which is face up.

In performance, approach Hector, fanning the cards face down from hand to hand. (Make sure you don't get too close to the bottom and tip off the red-backed card.) "Hector, I might spread the cards like this and have you choose a card. But this might give you a better choice."

Place the deck on the table and do the *Crisscross Force* (page 19). There's a difference, however. After the spectator cuts off a portion and places the other portion on top crosswise, you stall for a moment. Then you pick up the *top pile* of the crisscrossed cards. Take off the bottom card of this group and, without looking at its face, hand it face down to Hector. In our example, this is the blue-backed jack of hearts. "Take a look at your card, Hector, and show it around."

Meanwhile, put the pile you're holding on top of the other pile. Even the cards and pick them up. Hold the deck in the dealing position and tell Hector, "Push your card into the deck, please." He probably won't be able to push it all the way in, so you might have to push the card even with the others.

"I will now attempt an almost impossible feat. I'm going to try to make your card turn face up in the deck. What was your card, Hector?" He names it. Riffle the ends of the deck. Fan through to the face-up jack of hearts. "There it is—face up!" Take it from the deck and place it face up on the table. When the murmurs of approval die down, say, "What more could a magician do?"

Spread the deck face down next to the face-up jack of hearts. "Maybe I could change the color of the back!" Snap your fingers and turn the jack of hearts over, displaying its red back in contrast to the blue-backed deck.

Immediately pick up the deck; you don't want anyone going through it just now. Pick up the red-backed jack of hearts and put it into your pocket. Proceed with other tricks. If, as you're doing your routine, someone points out the blue-backed jack of hearts, say, "Oh, yes, I brought it back. *And* I changed it back to a blue-backed card." Then move right along.

FOUR ACES

♦ *It's Out of My Hands* ♦

How about yet another trick in which the spectator does all the work? Sprinkled among others, such tricks seem to be especially magical.

Edgar is an excellent card player, so you might ask him to take the deck and shuffle it. Continue: "Please go through the cards and take out the four aces."

When Edgar turns the deck face up, take note of the bottom card and remember it; this is your key card. Then you banter with the group, paying no particular attention as he tosses the aces out. (If he somehow manages to change the bottom card, however, take note of the new bottom card. This is your key card).

The aces are face up on the table. Ask Edgar to turn the deck face down. "Now, Edgar, put the aces in a face-down row, and then deal three cards on top of each ace." When he finishes, say, "Gather the piles up, one on top of the other, and put them on top of the deck."

Then: "Please give the deck a complete cut." Make sure that, as he begins the cut, he lifts off at least 16 cards. Usually, the completed cut will leave the aces somewhere around the middle of the deck.

"In a moment, we're going to make some piles, Edgar. Which pile would you prefer—pile 1, pile 2, pile 3, or pile 4?" Whatever he replies, repeat his choice so that everyone will remember.

"Please deal the cards slowly into a face-up pile. If all goes well, I'll get a strong feeling as to when you should stop."

At a certain point (described below) you tell him to stop. Then: "Deal the next four cards into a face-down row. Then deal the next four cards into a row, right on top of the first four cards. Do the same with the next four cards, and then four more." Make sure he deals the cards across in a row each time. As he deals each group of four, count, "One, two, three, four."

Call the group's attention once more to the number of the pile that Edgar chose. "Don't forget. At no time have I touched the cards. Would you please turn over the pile you picked." He does so, and there are the four aces.

How you do it: When Edgar deals the cards out face up, you know exactly where to stop him. You watch for your key card, the original bottom card of the deck. To make sure the aces get into the proper pile, you simply subtract the number of the chosen pile from 4. For instance, if Edgar chooses pile 4, you subtract 4 from 4, getting zero. After he turns over the key card, you allow no more cards to be dealt out face up. He immediately begins forming the four piles.

If he chooses pile 3, you subtract 3 from 4, getting 1. So you let one more card be dealt face up after the key card.

If he chooses 2, you subtract 2 from 4, getting 2. Therefore, two more cards are dealt after the key card.

If he chooses 1, you subtract 1 from 4, getting 3. So three more cards are dealt after the key card.

◆ *An Ace Collection* ◆

I particularly enjoy tricks in which the "dirty work" is over before you've barely begun. This old four-ace trick, which I have modified somewhat, is a good example.

Fan through the deck, faces towards yourself, looking for the aces. "I'll need four aces for this experiment," you explain. As you find each ace, slip it to the face (bottom) of the deck. Spread out the aces on the bottom, showing them. "Here are the aces. And I can assure you that these are the only aces in the deck." Continue fanning through the cards. After you fan off three more cards, hold all seven cards slightly apart from the rest with your right fingers (Illus. 17). Don't pause, but continue fanning through several more cards.

**7 cards are held apart
from the rest of the deck.**

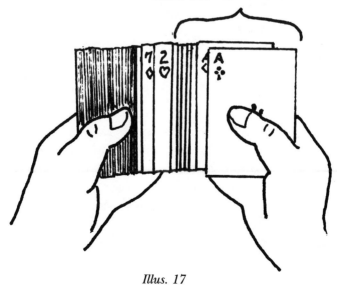

Illus. 17

Casually close up the cards, letting your right fingers slide under all seven cards at the face of the deck. Immediately lower your left hand and flip the rest of the deck over with your left thumb. Place the left side of the face-up packet that's in your right hand on the tips of the left fingers (Illus. 18). Flip this packet over with the tips of your *right* fingers, so that it falls face down on top of the deck. This whole casual sequence takes just a few seconds.

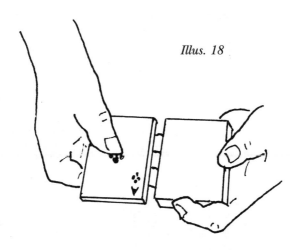

Illus. 18

As you go through the moves, say, "Now what we're going to do is . . ." By this time you should have completed the sequence. ". . . mix the aces . . ." Tap the top of the deck. ". . . throughout the deck."

Set the deck on the table and turn to Hedda. "I'll need your help, Hedda. Would you please cut the deck into two fairly even piles. But don't forget which is the top bunch."

She cuts the deck into two piles. Point to the original top group. "And this is the top group, right?"

Right. "Now would you cut each of *those* piles into two fairly even piles." She does. Again, point to the original top group. "And this is the group that was on top."

Pick up that pile. "Now let's distribute the aces." Deal one card from the top of the pile you're holding onto each of the other three piles. (Presumably, an ace is now on top of each pile; actually, all four aces are on top of the pile you're holding.) Set this pile down, alongside the other three.

"Let's make sure those aces are separated. Hedda, I'd like you to put these piles together in any order you wish. Just put one pile on top of the other until you have one pile."

After she finishes, have Hedda, or other spectators, give the deck any number of complete cuts.

Pick up the deck, saying, "It's magic time!" Riffle the ends of the cards. Turn the deck face up and fan through the cards, showing that the aces are all together.

◆ *Double or Nothing* ◆

I believe that the basic principle used here was developed by
Stewart James, and Ray Boston adapted it to a four-ace trick.
My version creates great spectator interest and has an ex-
tremely strong climax.

Start by tossing the four aces face up onto the table. "Here
we have the four aces, as you can see. Now I'm about to play
a game of *Double or Nothing.* I'll give out real money to the
winner. Whoever volunteers will risk nothing whatever. Do I
have a volunteer?"

You choose Hannibal from the multitude of eager volunteers.

"Congratulations, Hannibal. Just by volunteering, you
have already won. To win even more, you'll have to keep
track of the aces."

Arrange the aces in a face-down row. Fan off three cards
from the top of the deck and place them on top of one of
the aces. Tap the pile of four cards. "For double or nothing,
keep track of this ace, Hannibal."

Place the pile of four cards on top of the deck. As you do
so, get a break with your left little finger beneath the top
card of the four. Double-cut this card to the bottom of the
deck. (See *Double-Cut,* page 8.)

"Where's that first ace, Hannibal? Is it on the bottom?"
Turn the deck over, showing the bottom card. "No. Is it on
top?" Turn over the top card, showing it, and then turn it
face down again. "No. So where is it?" You coach Hannibal
by saying, "Somewhere in the mmmm . . . somewhere in the
mid . . ." Whatever he responds, you say, "Right! Somewhere
in the middle of the deck. You've doubled your money! You
now have *two* . . . pennies." This should get a chuckle. "Double or nothing, Hannibal. Let's try four pennies." Fan off the
top three cards and place them on another ace. Pick up the

four cards and place them on top of the deck. Double-cut the top card to the bottom of the deck.

"Where's that ace, Hannibal? Is it on the bottom?" Show the bottom card, as before. "No. Is it on top?" Show the top card and replace it. "No. So where is it?" Hannibal should have no trouble this time. "That's right," you say, "somewhere in the middle of the deck. You now have eight pennies. Let's try for 16."

The procedure this time is a little different. Fan off three cards from the top of the deck and place them on top of one of the two remaining aces. Pick up the four-card pile. Carefully even it up; you're going to turn the pile face up and you don't want anyone to get a glimpse of the other aces in the pile. *Now* turn the pile over, showing the ace on the bottom. Place the pile face down on top of the deck. "You *must* know where that ace is. Obviously, it isn't on the bottom." Show the bottom card of the deck, as before. "And it isn't on top." Show the top card and return it to the top.

At this point, double-cut the top card to the bottom. "So, for 16 pennies, where is it?" As usual, it's somewhere in the middle of the deck.

"The last double-or-nothing." Fan off the top three cards and place them on the last ace on the table. Place the four cards on top of the deck. "For 32 pennies, Hannibal—where are all four aces?"

Chances are he'll say, "In the middle of the deck." If he does, say, "Not exactly. They're right here." Deal off the top four cards face up. They are the aces. (Whatever he responds, proceed the same way.)

Pause a moment for audience appreciation. "But that was close enough, Hannibal. You still win the 32 pennies." Take out your wallet. "Do you have change for a big bill?"

◆ *Wally's Wily Ace Trick* ◆

Wally Wilson was kind enough to give me permission to use his simplified and surprising version of an excellent four-ace trick. What's unique about this effect is that no one knows it's a four-ace trick until the very end.

In the original version, some preparation was necessary. I have changed things a bit so that the trick can be done impromptu. (You may prefer to do the other version, which I fully explain in the *Note* at the end.) We will assume that some time earlier you performed a four-ace trick so that the four aces are together somewhere in the deck. Casually fan through the deck and cut the four aces to the top.

Estelle enjoys a good card trick, so approach her, saying, "Believe it or not, Estelle, I've just memorized the position of every single card in the deck. Let's see if I can prove it to you." As you say this, fan the cards face down from hand to hand, counting them. When you reach the 12th card, hold it, along with the cards above it, separate from the rest; continue fanning through the cards. "Please pick one out, Estelle." After she takes a card, close the cards up, getting a break with your left little finger beneath that 12th card. (It's best to count the cards in groups of three, thinking to yourself, "Three, six, nine, twelve.")

"Show the card around, please."

Grip the deck with the right hand from above, transferring the left little-finger break to the right thumb (Illus. 19). The thumb break is on the right side of the deck. The first finger of the right hand is holding the cards down so that no separation will be apparent to the spectators.

Riffle your left thumb down the left side of the deck all the way to the bottom (Illus. 20). Start to riffle the cards again, but stop when your thumb reaches a point about a third down in the deck. Lift off the top 12 cards with your

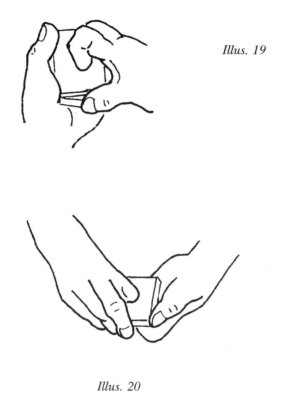

Illus. 19

Illus. 20

right hand. Hold out the lower portion with your left hand for the return of the chosen card. If Estelle hesitates, say, "Just put it right there, please." After she places her card on top of the pile, replace the 12-card packet. This time you don't hold a break. Her card is now 13th from the top of the deck.

"Contrary to what you may have heard, Estelle, I'm a very observant person. For instance, I happen to know that your card is in the top half of the deck. So we won't need all these cards."

Deal three cards from the top of the deck, one at a time, into a pile. To the right of these, deal another pile of three cards, also one at a time. Go back to the first pile and deal a card on top of it. Do the same with the pile on the right. Continue alternating until you have two 13-card piles. (Count silently, of course.) At the end, you are holding half the deck. Turn over the top card of these. Let's say that it's a red card. If you choose, you may now use one of Wally Wilson's clever lines. Say to Estelle, "Your card was a red card, was it not?" If she says yes, fine. If she says no, say, "Well, I said it was not."

Regardless, replace the card face down and set down the half deck you're holding so that it's well out of the way.

At this point, the pile on your left has three aces on the bottom; the pile on your right has one ace on the bottom. You must arrange it so that the left pile has *two* aces on the bottom and an ace second from the top. And the right pile must have its ace on top. Here's how you manage it: Point to the two 13-card piles. "So, Estelle, I know that your card is in one of these piles." Pick up the pile on the left. Hold it from above in the left hand (Illus. 21). With the right thumb on top and the right fingers below, grasp the top and bottom cards together and pull them sideways from the packet (Illus. 22). "Your card could be the top or bottom card of this packet," you say. "*Apparently,* I have no way of knowing." Place the two cards on top of the deck. Fan the cards out. "More than likely, your card is somewhere in the middle. *If* it's in this pile." Close up the packet and set it onto the table. That pile is set. What's more, the chosen card is in proper position.

Pick up the packet on the right. Casually give it an overhand shuffle, shuffling off the last few cards singly so that the bottom card ends up on top. "Of course, your card might be somewhere in here." Fan the packet out. "Who knows?"

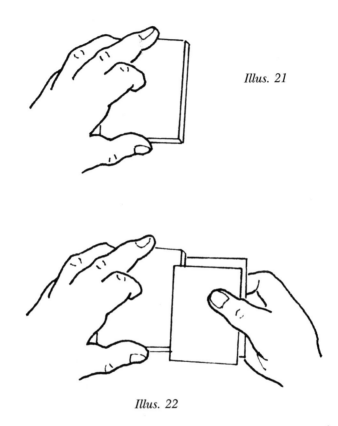

Illus. 21

Illus. 22

Close the packet up and return it to the table. This pile is also set.

Place one hand above each pile, twitching your fingers and staring into the distance. Pick up the pile on the right and place it to one side. Indicate the pile under your left hand. "It must be in this pile."

Pick up the pile and, going from left to right, deal it one card at a time alternately into two piles. The pile on the left contains seven cards, and the pile on the right six cards. Toss in appropriate patter about trying to sense which pile contains the chosen card as you again place your hands over the two piles. Eventually, you pick up the pile on the left and place it right next to the first pile you discarded. Indicate that the small pile remaining under your right hand contains the chosen card.

Pick up this six-card pile and deal it into two piles, as before. This time each pile contains three cards. This time, you eliminate the pile on the right. Place it near the other two discarded piles.

"So we're down to three cards." Deal them out alternately from left to right. On your left is a two-card pile, which, after the usual rigmarole, you place aside with the other discarded piles. On your right is one card. "This must be the one you chose, Estelle. What's the name of your card?"

She names it, and you turn it over. You're absolutely right. But you may not receive the praise and applause you're entitled to. After a pause, you say, "Well, if you didn't care for that demonstration, perhaps you'd like to see something with the four aces."

Turn over the top card of each of the discarded piles. They are, of course, the four aces.

It's easy to remember which pile you must set aside: The first time, you set aside the pile on the right; next, the pile on the left; then the pile on the right; and finally the pile on the left. In other words, you first discard the pile on the right, and then alternate.

Wally's Setup Version: You may prefer to have the deck set up in advance. If so, the four aces must be distributed like this: on top of the deck, 3rd from the top, 23rd from the top, and 26th from the top.

Approach Estelle, fanning the cards and saying, "I could offer you the choice of a card by letting you pick one from the deck, Estelle. But let's do something a little different."

As you fan the cards, count off the top *eleven*. When you reach the 11th card, close the cards up, getting a break with your left little finger beneath that card. (Count the cards in groups of three, thinking to yourself, "Three, six, nine, and two more.")

Still holding the break, grasp the deck with the right hand from above (refer to Illus. 19). Riffle your left thumb down the left side of the deck all the way to the bottom (refer to Illus. 20). "Just tell me when to stop, Estelle," you say, starting to riffle your thumb down again, slowly this time. If she says stop somewhere in the top third of the deck, fine. If not, riffle rapidly all the way down. "Let's try again," you say with a smile. When Estelle does stop you in the top third of the deck, lift off the top eleven cards with your right hand. Show the card to her (Illus. 23), saying, "Please remember this card, Estelle." Replace the packet on top of the deck. This time you don't hold a break. All the "dirty work" is done.

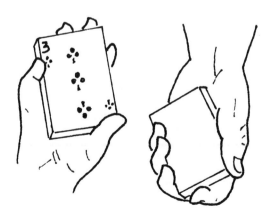

Illus. 23

You do not shift the aces around as in the first version. Simply deal the cards into two piles of 13 cards each, alternating from left to right. As in the first version, first eliminate the pile on the right, then the pile on the left, and so on, alternating.

Mental Magic

♦ *How Lucky Can You Get!* ♦

I love this trick. It has strong spectator participation and a striking climax. The originator is Graham Cheminais. I've changed the handling.

Ask Cliff and Roberta to assist you in a mental experiment. Yes, you, with your magnificently omniscient mind, are going to attempt to tell the future.

Have Cliff shuffle the deck. Take the cards back and hold them with the faces towards you. "I'm going to remove a card which *may* prove that I've foretold the future. Notice that I do not change the position of any cards."

Very deliberately begin fanning the cards from the top of the deck—the portion farthest from you. Note the 4th card from the top. Continue fanning through until you come to the card that matches it in color and value. Let's say that the 4th card from the top is the queen of clubs; you fan through the deck until you come to the queen of spades. Remove this card from the deck and hold it face down.

"Roberta, would you please hold out your hand palm up?" Place the card on her hand. "Please guard that for me until later. No peeking, now!"

Set the deck onto the table. "Cliff, please cut off about half the cards and place the cut-off portion here." Point to a position at least 8 inches to the left of the bottom portion of the deck. "Now cut off about half of each of these piles

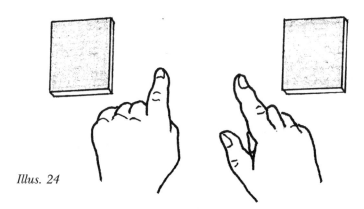

Illus. 24

and place them here.'' With both forefingers, point to positions between the two piles (Illus. 24). There are now four piles on the table. The second pile from your left is the original top portion of the deck. The 4th card from the top of this pile matches the card that Roberta is holding. In our example, the 4th card from the top is the queen of clubs, and Roberta is holding the queen of spades.

Using the simplest method possible, you now force your assistants to choose the second pile from your left. Place your right hand on top of the two piles on your right, and place your left hand on top of the two piles on your left (Illus. 25). ''Roberta,'' you say, ''right or left?'' Whatever she responds, say, ''All right,'' and pull the two piles on your right towards you.

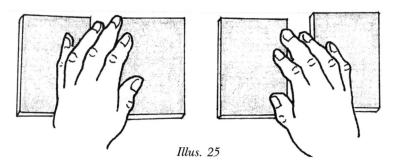

Illus. 25

"Cliff, hand me one of the other two piles." If he hands you the pile containing the queen of clubs, say, "Fine," and place the pile in front of him. Draw back the remaining pile so that it is in a row with the other two. If, instead, he hands you the pile which does not contain the queen of clubs, say, "Fine," and place this pile so that it is in a row with the two you drew back. In either instance, he has the proper pile in front of him while the other three piles are in a row (Illus. 26).

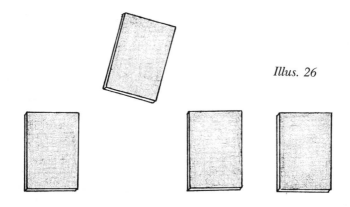

Illus. 26

"Roberta, would you please hold out your other hand palm up?"

Turn to Cliff. "Please pick up your pile and deal one card on top of each of the other piles. Then deal the next card face down onto Roberta's hand."

After he finishes, say, "Let's see if the cards match. Roberta, would you show the two cards?"

She holds the two cards up, displaying a perfect match. You might murmur, "I can't believe how lucky I am!"

◆ *The Super Dupe Trick* ◆

The original trick was by Bob Brethen, reported by Bob Hades. It required ESP cards. I have changed that, along with some other particulars. The result is an amusing "sucker" trick, which is totally impromptu.

Announce: "Let's try an exercise in ESP. I'll try to control your minds so that you'll choose the very cards I want you to. First, I'll need certain cards."

Fan through the deck, faces towards yourself. Toss onto the table face down six red cards (a mix of hearts and diamonds): 2, 3, 4, 5, 6, 8. Also, toss out face down the two black 7s. If you are tossing the cards into a pile, the only essential is that the two black 7s be third and fourth from the top. You then deal the cards into a face-down row, from left to right. A typical layout, from left to right, might be this:

2H   3D   7C   7S   4H   5H   6D   8D

(If you prefer, you can simply toss the cards at random face down onto the table and then lay them out, making sure that the two black 7s occupy the positions shown.)

"I will need two assistants." Brenda and Christopher are kind enough to volunteer.

"Christopher, we have eight cards here. So in a moment I'd like you to name a number from 1 to 8. When you name your number, we'll spell it out—not count it, spell it. Which would you prefer—an odd number or an even number?" He selects odd or even. "All right. Now what number do you choose?"

Whatever number he names, you spell it out so that you land on one of the 7s. You either start on the left and move to the right, touching one card for each letter in the spelling; or you start on the right and move to the left, touching one card for each letter in the spelling. O-N-E, T-W-O, F-O-U-R,

F-I-V-E, and S-I-X are all spelled from your left to right. T-H-R-E-E, S-E-V-E-N, and E-I-G-H-T are all spelled from your right to left.

Whichever 7 you land on, push it well forward of the group. "So this is the card that Christopher chose. But we won't look at it just yet."

Arrange the remaining cards so that the open space is filled. Let's say that the 7C was chosen. The remaining layout is this:

2H   3D   7S   4H   5H   6D   8D

Brenda will now choose a number, but if she chooses the number 4, it will neither count nor spell out. That's why you had Christopher choose odd or even. Now, regardless of what Christopher chose, you'll have Brenda choose an odd number—like this:

"Brenda, we have only seven cards left, so you'll have to choose a number from 1 to 7. But this time we'll do it differently." This last sentence is to cover the possibility that you may have to start from the other end, or count instead of spell.

Now if Christopher had chosen an odd number, you continue, "So please choose an odd number from 1 to 7." If he had chosen an even number, you say, "Since Christopher chose an even number, you'll pick an odd number. So name an odd number from 1 to 7."

Since the remaining 7 is 3rd from the left in the row, you can reach it with any odd number by either spelling or *counting*. You've already said that you'll do it differently, so it makes no difference if you start spelling from the other direction. Nor does it matter whether you have to count instead of spell. In fact, it's best not to mention it. Just go ahead and spell or count, depending on the number she chooses.

O-N-E is spelled from left to right. T-H-R-E-E and S-E-V-E-N are spelled from right to left. The number 5 must be *counted* from right to left.

So you land on the other black 7. Push this card forward so that it's with the other 7.

"Christopher and Brenda have chosen two cards at random. Wouldn't it be amazing if the two cards matched?" Turn the two cards over. "They *do* match. It's a miracle!" Blather on about this incredible coincidence; offer to present another demonstration of a different nature. Eventually, many will express curiosity about the cards that were not chosen. Feign reluctance: "There's no point in looking at these cards. What difference does it make?" Finally, turn the cards over. "No . . . no matches here. All red, and all different values."

♦ *27-Card Trick* ♦

You deal out three rows with seven cards in each row. A spectator thinks of one of the cards. You gather up the piles and make sure the pile in which his card appears is in the middle. You repeat this twice. When you gather up the cards the last time, the chosen card is 11th from the top.

Sound familiar? Of course. For thousands of people, this is the one card trick that they can do.

An old variation of this trick involved 27 cards, and the magician brought the chosen card to a selected number in the group. It's an excellent trick, but it hasn't been performed often because it requires either considerable memorization or a cheat-sheet. But I, with my infinite persistence, have worked out a simpler method of calculation which makes it possible for even me, with my finite memory, to do the trick.

Here's the effect: Have Bea shuffle the deck. You take the cards and deal them into three face-down piles of nine cards each, counting aloud as you deal each pile. Have Bea pick up a pile and, while you avert your head, think of one of the cards therein. She replaces the pile onto the table.

Another spectator gives you a number from 1 to 27. You tell everyone, "Please remember that number; it'll become very important later on."

Form the three piles into one pile. Then distribute the cards like this: Deal three cards in a face-up row from left to right. Then deal three more across on top of these, overlapping downwards so that the values of the top row can still be seen. Continue until all 27 cards have been dealt. Ask Bea in which row her card appears. Gather up the three rows. Turn the packet face down and repeat the entire procedure. Finally, ask if anyone remembers what number had been chosen. Deal off a pile to that number and turn over the chosen card.

The secret, of course, lies in how the piles are gathered. The pile in which the chosen card lies is placed in one of three positions:

Position 1: On top of the other two piles. (This means that it is the top pile when the cards are turned face down.)

Position 2: Between the other two piles.

Position 3: Below the other two piles. (This means that it is the bottom pile when the cards are turned face down.)

You have just counted off three piles of nine cards each, and Bea has looked through one pile to think of a card. Does this pile go into Position 1, 2, or 3? It depends on the number chosen by the other spectator.

1st Placement: Divide the chosen number by 3. If it divides evenly, the selected pile goes into Position 3. If it does not divide evenly, note the remainder. If the remainder is 1, the selected pile goes into Position 1. If the remainder is 2, the selected pile goes into Position 2.

Let's say in our example with Bea that the chosen number is 19. Divide 3 into 19 and you get 6, with a remainder of 1. Since the remainder is 1, the selected pile goes into Position 1.

You turn the 27-card packet face down and, from the top, deal three columns of cards face up, as described above. Bea indicates which of these contains her card. Where does this pile go?

2nd Placement: If the chosen number is not a single digit, reduce it to a single digit by adding the digits together. For instance, if the chosen number is 25, add the 2 and the 5, getting 7. If the result is 1, 2, or 3, the selected pile goes into Position 1. If the result is 4, 5, or 6, the selected pile goes into Position 2. If the result is 7, 8, or 9, the selected pile goes into Position 3. This chart may help:

$$1, 2, 3 = \text{Position 1}$$
$$4, 5, 6 = \text{Position 2}$$
$$7, 8, 9 = \text{Position 3}$$

In our example with Bea, the chosen number is 19. Add the 1 and the 9, getting 10. Add the 1 and the zero, getting 1. So the selected pile goes into Position 1.

The cards are dealt out once more, and once more Bea indicates which pile contains her card.

3rd Placement: If the chosen number is 1 to 9, the selected pile goes into Position 1. If the chosen number is 10 to 18, the selected pile goes into Position 2. If the chosen number is 19 to 27, the selected pile goes into Position 3. This chart may help:

$$1 \text{ to } 9 = \text{Position 1}$$
$$10 \text{ to } 18 = \text{Position 2}$$
$$19 \text{ to } 27 = \text{Position 3}$$

In our example with Bea, the chosen number is 19, so the selected pile goes into Position 3.

After you gather up the cards for the last time, even them up and ask, "Does anyone remember the chosen number?" You then deal that number of cards into a pile. Ask Bea the name of her card. Turn over the last card dealt.

Let's try another example. Lydia shuffles the cards and deals three piles of nine cards each. She picks up one of the piles and thinks of one of the cards therein. Another spectator volunteers the number 8.

You divide 3 into 8, getting 2, with a remainder of 2. Since the remainder is 2, you place the selected pile into Position 2.

The cards are dealt out in three face-up columns. Lydia tells you which one contains her card. (1, 2, or 3 is Position 1; 4, 5, or 6 is Position 2; 7, 8, or 9 is Position 3.) The chosen number is 8, so you place the selected pile into Position 3.

Again the cards are dealt out in three face-up columns. Lydia tells you which one her card is in. (1 to 9 is Position 1; 10 to 18 is Position 2; 19 to 27 is Position 3.) The chosen number is 8, so you place the selected pile into Position 1.

After the cards are gathered, you ask again for the chosen number. You count off eight cards. The chosen one is the last one dealt.

Note: Since the placements are progressive, I find them easy to remember. We start with the number 3, go to three sets of three, and end with three sets of nine. You might think of it this way:

(1) Divide by 3. If it's even, it's 3. Otherwise, use the remainder.

(2) 3, 6, 9 for Positions 1, 2, 3.

(3) 9, 18, 27 for Positions 1, 2, 3.

◆ *The Misguided Spectator* ◆

At a meeting of magicians in a restaurant, I saw a young magician doing a trick for a young lady. "Think of a card," he said. She did. He removed a card from his deck and placed it face down on the table. "What's your card?" he asked. She named it. He began stalling, trying to figure out what to do. Apparently, his 52 to 1 shot had not worked out. I felt a bit uncomfortable, so I left, hoping that he would work out an adequate solution.

Later, I worked out my own solution, which I passed on to the young man. He seemed to like it. Since then, I've frequently performed the trick; spectators find it amusing and surprising.

In my experience a woman will fairly often choose the ace of hearts. So I suggest that you perform the trick for a woman—Stephanie, for instance—and that you start by placing the ace of hearts face down on the table. "Stephanie, please name any card in the deck."

She does. If she names the ace of hearts, you have a miracle. But the chances are overwhelming that she won't. So, in response to whatever other card she names, you say, "Excellent!" But a good magician must build suspense.

Fan through the deck, faces towards yourself, looking for the card. After you fan five or six cards, cut these to the top. Continue this cutting procedure with small groups of cards. When you come to the named card, let's say the six of diamonds, cut the cards you have fanned off to the back of the deck, thus bringing the card to the face of the deck. Fan through several more cards. "No, I guess I did it right." Close up the cards and turn the deck face down. Make sure, of course, that no one gets a glimpse of the card on the bottom.

Point to the card on the table. "I not only have your card here . . . a miracle in itself . . ." Drop the deck directly onto the card on the table. ". . . but I'm going to cause it to rise to the top of the deck."

Stephanie is wondering, "What kind of a stupid trick is this? He put my card on top when he was fanning through the deck, and now he's going to pretend that it's going to appear there magically! What an idiot!"

You blithely proceed. Pick up the deck in your left hand in the glide grip (refer to *Glide*, page 20). Tap the top card with your right first finger. Turn the card over and drop it face up onto the table. "There it is!" Name the card you turned over. Stephanie now *knows* that you're an idiot. She already told you her card, and that isn't it. So she says, "No, it isn't. My card's the six of diamonds."

You say, "That's right . . . I forgot! How silly of me!"

While saying this, perform the glide, casually dropping the chosen card face down onto the table. *Immediately* pick up the face-up card and stick it, face down, into the middle of the deck, saying, "Let me try it again. I know I can do this."

Place the deck crosswise onto the card on the table so that at least one third of the back of the chosen card shows. "Watch, Stephanie. I'll bring your card to the top." Tap the top card of the deck. Say, "Now I want you, yourself, to turn the top card over."

Again you've failed to bring the chosen card to the top. Express chagrin. "Well, at least I knew what card you were going to choose, and that's really the hard part. Now let me show you something else . . ." Do not touch the cards, but blather on until it finally occurs to Stephanie that she'd like to look at the card you predicted. Tell her to go ahead. Sure enough, your prediction was right.

The misdirection on this trick is just about perfect; spectators are so intent on your absurd failures that they miss the sleight completely.

◆ *Mix and Match* ◆

A wonderful prediction trick depended on having *two decks* completely set up. I thought that, using the same principle, I could *easily* come up with a completely impromptu version. I was wrong about *easily;* the word I needed was *eventually.*

"Ladies and gentlemen," you announce, "I am about to attempt a feat of prognostication. And, if that doesn't work out, I'll just try to predict the future. Which, by the way, is a lot harder than trying to predict the past. We'll use this deck of cards."

Hand the deck to Chelsea as you implore her to help you out. "Chelsea, will you please remove from the deck all the clubs. Just put them in a pile here." Indicate a spot on the table.

We'll assume that Chelsea puts the clubs into a face-up pile. If she doesn't, you do so. They will be in random order. "Let's make sure you got them all," you say, as you spread the pile out so that you can see the values of all the cards. Go over them from low to high, announcing each value as you see it.

Take the rest of the deck from Chelsea. Say, "I'll need one card of each value also. But it'll go faster if I just take a variety of suits." You now form a face-down packet of 13 cards in which the values run exactly opposite to those in Chelsea's pile. Look at Chelsea's first four cards—the ones which would be on top of the packet if her cards were face down. Let's suppose these are the 8, 6, K, and 3 of clubs. You find any 8 and place it face down onto the table. Now you find a 6 and place it on top of your 8. You do the same with a K, and then a 3. Later, when you turn Chelsea's packet face down, her four top cards, in order, will be 8, 6, K, and 3. Your bottom card will be an 8, the one above it a 6, above that a K, and above that a 3.

Note Chelsea's next four cards. As you do so, mutter, "I have to make sure I get one of each value." Match these cards, just as you did before. Continue until your pile precisely matches Chelsea's, only in reverse order.

Note and remember the top card of Chelsea's packet, which matches the bottom card of your packet. In our example, the card is an 8.

Close up Chelsea's packet, turn it face down, and place it in front of her. Even up your pile, saying, "Now my packet must be cut exactly three times. It's not that three is a mystical number—which it is. It's just that I *like* the number three. Chelsea, would you give my packet a complete cut."

Have someone else give the packet a second cut, and then have Chelsea cut it again. Fan your packet out, faces towards you, saying, "Now I'm going to cut a special card to a certain position in my packet." You bet you are; in fact, you're going to cut the original bottom card back to the bottom. In this instance, take all the cards below the 8 and place them on top, making the 8 the bottom card. Once more, your packet is set up precisely opposite to Chelsea's. "If all goes well, I've correctly predicted which card you'll choose. If not . . . I'm still a nice person."

Set your packet onto the table. Pick up Chelsea's packet. "If it's all right with you, we're going to try this experiment twice. In a moment I'm going to deal these cards one by one into a pile. To make sure everything's on the up-and-up, I'm going to deal the cards face up. But first, I have to know: Do you prefer odd numbers or even numbers?"

If she prefers odd numbers, say, "Then please pick an odd number between 1 and 13." If she prefers even numbers, say, "Then please pick an even number between 1 and 13."

Suppose Chelsea chooses an odd number, let's say 5. You deal one less than that number into a face-up pile, counting aloud. As you count five, you place the fifth card face up to the right of the dealt pile. Turn the dealt pile face down. Pick up the face-up card which you placed next to the pile. Put it, still face up, on top of the pile. Place the cards left in your hand on top of all.

If Chelsea chooses an even number, the procedure is slightly different. Suppose she chooses 8. You count eight cards into a face-up pile. Turn the pile face down. Take the *next card* from the deck and turn it face up. Place this card onto the pile on the table. Place the remaining cards in your hand on top of all.

In both instances, you even up her pile and announce, "So, Chelsea, your card is face up in the middle of this pile."

Remember: The card which you turn over must be an odd number from the top.

On with the trick: Set her pile on the table so that it is side by side with your pile. Simultaneously lift off the top cards. Turn them over, showing them, and then set them aside face down. The card in your left hand goes to the left of its pile, and the card in your right hand goes to the right of its pile. As you show the cards, say, "These two don't match in value." Turn over the next top cards the same way, and place them face down on top of the previous discards. Say, "No match here." Continue until you come to the face-up card. Take it and the corresponding card from your pile and place them in front of their respective piles. Chelsea's card stays face up, and yours remains face down. Say, "Here's your card, along with my prediction."

Go through the rest of the packets, each time saying something like, "No match." Note the last card shown in Chelsea's packet.

Turn over your "prediction card," setting it next to the face-up card. "But here we *do* have a match. So my prediction actually worked out."

At this point you can quit, having performed a very effective trick. It may be even more effective, however, if you do it again.

Pause a moment. "But let's try it again to make sure it wasn't mere coincidence."

Take Chelsea's face-up card and place it face down on the bottom of her packet. Set the packet face down in front of her.

You have noted the last card shown in Chelsea's packet, now her top card. Let's suppose that card was the 10. Pick up your packet and fan through the cards, faces towards yourself. Pick up your prediction card and put it into the packet on the near side of the 10. (When your packet is turned face down, your original prediction card will be the card below the 10.) As you put the card in, say, "We'd better get rid of this."

Set your packet face down onto the table. Once more it gets cut three times. And again you fan through to "cut a special card to a certain position." In this instance, you cut the 10 (the match to the top card of Chelsea's packet) to the bottom. Your packet is now in reverse order to that of Chelsea.

"Now let's try it again. You prefer odd numbers (or even numbers), so pick another number between 1 and 13. Or, if you prefer, you may pick the same one."

Proceed with the trick exactly as before.

Note: The above is the simplest way to perform the trick. You may prefer a somewhat more difficult method, which apparently gives the spectator greater freedom of choice.

After you've cut your packet so that it matches Chelsea's in reverse order, tell her, "I'm going to deal your pile into a face-up pile. Your job is to stop me whenever you wish."

Very deliberately deal cards from the packet face up into a pile. Silently keep count. Chelsea tells you to stop. You stop dealing immediately. "Right there, or do you want me to deal more?" If she wants you to deal more, continue your silent count, for you must know whether the number dealt is odd or even. The procedure is different for each.

Suppose Chelsea stops you after there is an *odd number* of face-up cards on the table. Follow this procedure *exactly:* Pick up the last card dealt (which is face up, of course) with your right hand and place it face up on top of the packet in your left hand. Turn the packet that's on the table face down. You need to distract the spectators for a brief period to help them forget exactly what is happening. You do this with "time misdirection." Make eye-contact with Chelsea and say, "You chose the place to stop."

With your right hand, take the face-up card from the top of the packet you're holding and place it face up onto the packet on the table. With your right hand, take the packet from your left hand and place it face down on top of the packet on the table. Even up the packet. "So, Chelsea, your card is face up in the middle of this pile."

Suppose Chelsea stops you after there is an *even number* of face-up cards on the table. You will follow a similar, but different procedure. Take off the top card of those you're holding in your left hand. Turn it face up and return it to the top of the pile you're holding. With your right hand, turn the pile on the table face down. Make eye-contact with Chelsea and say, "You chose this place to stop."

Take the face-up card from the top of the packet you're holding and place it face up on top of the packet on the table. With your right hand, take the packet from your left hand and place it on top of the packet on the table. Even up the packet, saying, "So, Chelsea, your card is face up in the middle of this pile."

You then complete the trick as described above, including a repeat.

Why this attention to detail? If you only do the trick once, it doesn't matter. If you do the trick twice, and each time Chelsea stops you at an even number, it doesn't matter. And if each time she stops you at an odd number, it doesn't matter. But if she stops you at an odd number the first time, and an even number the second time, or vice versa, the procedures must *appear* to be the same.

GAMBLING

♦ *Freedom of Choice* ♦

I hit upon the basic principle used here some time ago, but only recently developed a trick that takes full advantage of it. This trick has been well received by magicians and laypersons alike.

Since Evan likes card games, say to him, "Let's see how good a poker player you are. First, would you please shuffle the deck." After he finishes, take the deck back, and turn it face up so that all can see the cards. "Evan, I'm going to try to find you a really bad five-card poker hand. *But* I'll give you a bonus card. First, we'll take the bottom card." Name the card at the face of the deck. Suppose it is the two of clubs. Say, "So the two of clubs is your first card."

Proceed to fan through the cards, ostensibly choosing a five-card hand for Evan, along with a bonus card. As you do this, you will be placing five face-up piles onto the table. Unknown to the spectators, the second card from the bottom of each face-up pile will be a member of the spade royal flush (AS, KS, QS, JS, 10S). In other words, when each pile is turned face down, the second card from the top will be a member of the spade royal flush.

You have called attention to the two of clubs, the bottom card. "Let's find another good card for you." Fan through the cards until you come to a member of the spade royal flush. Fan off one additional card, calling attention to the card now at the face of those in your left hand. "Here's a really bad card," you say. "So this will be your second card" (Illus. 27). Even up the cards in your right hand and set them in a face-up pile on the table. In our example, the top card of this face-up pile is the two of clubs; the second card from the bottom of the face-up pile is part of the spade royal flush.

Illus. 27

In the same way, fan through to the next member of the spade royal flush. Again, fan off one additional card. Name the card at the face of those in your left hand and make a comment about it. Even up the cards in your right hand and place them in a face-up pile next to the other pile on the table.

Do this two more times. Four face-up piles are in a row on the table. The face card of each pile is one you have selected for the spectator's hand. The second card from the bottom of each face-up pile is a part of the spade royal flush. The face card of those in your left hand is the fifth card you have selected for the spectator. "Now," you say, "I'll give you a bonus card."

Again fan through the cards, going one beyond the last card of the spade royal flush. Perform the same routine, placing a fifth pile face up on the table, next to the others. The second card from the bottom of this face-up pile is the fifth card of the spade royal flush. The "bonus card" is at the face of those in your left hand.

(If you've been following along with a deck of cards, you may have run into some trouble. I deal with this in the *Notes* at the end.)

Gesture towards the piles on the table. "These five cards are your poker hand. If you want, you can exchange one of those for the bonus card. What could be fairer?"

If Evan chooses to make the exchange, trade the card at the face of those in your left hand for the face card of the face-up packet he chooses. Set the cards in your hand aside face down. If he chooses not to make the exchange, simply set the leftover cards aside face down.

Place the top card of each pile above its pile. You now have five face-up piles in a row. Above this is another row, consisting of individual face-up cards (Illus. 28). "Now you can exchange any of your cards for any of the new cards here." Evan does so, probably enhancing his hand considerably.

Illus. 28

"Now I'm *really* going to give you a break." Turn all five piles face down. Turn the top card of each pile face up on top of its pile. "You can exchange any of these cards to improve your hand." Now he should have an excellent hand.

Remove the leftover face-up cards from the five piles and toss them face down on top of the cards you set aside earlier.

"Do you have a good hand?" you ask Evan. Of course he does. "I agree. In fact, I think you'd win most card games with that hand. So let's see how *I* might do."

Turn over the top card of each pile. You win, for you have a royal flush in spades. "Not bad."

Notes

(1) As you fan through the cards, two members of the spade royal flush may be close together. When you notice this, cut between the two cards and give the deck a quick overhand shuffle. Then hand the deck to a spectator and have him shuffle "so that everything is perfectly fair." The trick is not diminished, even if this occurs more than once.

(2) Sometimes you'll fan through 15 to 20 cards without coming across a member of the spade royal flush. When this happens, comment, "I don't see anything I like here." Cut about 12 cards or so to the top and then continue the fanning procedure.

(3) Occasionally, in the fanning procedure, you'll provide the spectator some good cards—a pair of aces, for instance. When this occurs, say, "I'm feeling generous. I might as well give you a *few* good cards."

◆ *From the Land Down Under* ◆

Ken Beale created an unusual poker trick, to which I have added a strong climax and appropriate patter.

You must make a simple setup in advance. Place the four aces on top of the deck and a small straight flush on the bottom of the deck. A typical straight flush might be 5H, 6H, 7H, 8H, 9H. As you might know, a straight flush beats any other hand except a higher straight flush.

Look through the deck, faces towards yourself, and find the four jacks, tossing them face up onto the table. "Never play poker with a man from Australia," you say. "I met a fellow from Australia the other day. His name was Kangaroo Downs, and he invited me to play poker with him. The first thing he did was take the jacks from the deck. He said, 'In Australia, we always use the four jacks,' " Indicate the jacks on the table. "Then he said, 'In Australia, we play with just 16 cards, so we'll need 12 more cards.' Then he counted out 12 cards like this."

Fan out the top three cards. Remove them from the deck and place them into a pile on the table, saying, "Three." Fan off two more cards and place them on top of the pile of three, saying, "Five." Deal single cards onto the pile, counting aloud: "Six, seven, eight . . . ." When you reach 12, stop. Set the rest of the deck aside. Pick up the pile.

"Then Kangaroo Downs said, 'In Australia, we mix the cards like this.' " Turn the jacks face down so that they are in a row. Dealing from left to right, place one card on each jack. Repeat until all 12 cards are dealt out. Pick up the pile on the left. Place the pile to the right of it on top. Place the next pile to the right on top of the combined pile. And place the pile on the extreme right on top of all.

"Kangaroo said, 'In Australia, we always do a down-under deal, like this.' "

Deal the top card face down onto the table, saying, "Down." Place the next card on the bottom of the stack in your hand, saying, "Under." Deal the next card onto the card on the table, saying, "Down." The next card goes under. Continue the deal until four cards remain in your hand. But you can stop saying "Down" and "Under" about halfway through.

"Kangaroo handed me the remaining four cards. He said, 'Here's your hand.'

"I said, 'But a poker hand should be five cards.'

"He said, 'Not in Australia. Care to make a bet?' I looked at my hand."

You are holding the four jacks. Place them face up onto the table. "A very good hand. So I made a little wager. Kangaroo said, 'Now for my hand.' "

Pick up the cards on the table and do the down-under deal until four cards remain in your hand. "I showed him my four jacks. And he showed me his four aces."

Lay the aces face up onto the table. "Then Kangaroo said, 'Let that be a lesson to you: Never play the other fellow's game.'

"I said, 'True. But in all fairness, we should play one hand of American poker, double or nothing.'

"Kangaroo said, 'Okay. You can deal, but I get to shuffle Australian style.' I agreed. He gathered up the cards like this."

Pick up the cards you dealt onto the table and put them on top of the deck. Place the four jacks face down on top of the deck. Place the four aces face down on top of them.

(You can leave out the following shuffle if you wish.) "Kangaroo gave the deck a really sneaky shuffle." You perform a riffle-shuffle as follows: Take the top half of the deck in your left hand and the bottom half in your right hand. Riffle off at least a dozen cards with your left thumb before you start interweaving the cards in your right hand. At the end, you will automatically riffle off on top a dozen or so cards from your right hand. This means that your small straight flush remains on the bottom of the deck and the four aces remain on top.

"Kangaroo said, 'Now we'll do the down-under *shuffle.*' "

Hold the deck from above in your left hand (Illus. 29). With the right thumb on top and the right fingers below, grasp the top and bottom cards together and pull them sideways from the packet (Illus. 30). Set the pair onto the table. Take the top and bottom cards again in the same way. Set this pair on top of the first pair. Continue until you have 10 cards in the pile.

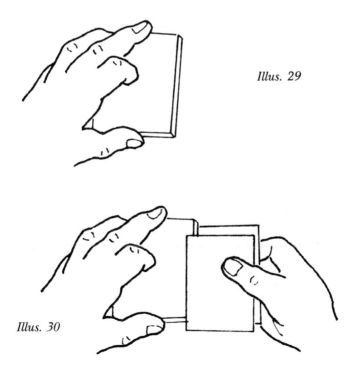

Illus. 29

Illus. 30

"Kangaroo said, 'Here are your 10 cards. Deal 'em!' So I took the 10 cards and dealt them like this."

Deal out two regular poker hands. The first card goes to your opponent, the second to yourself, and so on, until all ten are dealt.

"Kangaroo said, 'What do you know! I got the aces again.' "

Turn over his hand, showing the aces.

" 'Excellent hand,' I said. 'But I don't think it beats this.' "

Turn over your straight flush one card at a time.

"He was so angry, I figured the least I could do was offer some advice. I said, 'Let that be a lesson to you: Never play the other fellow's game.' "

◆ *Really Wild* ◆

I always liked this trick, the invention of Henry Christ. But it had what I considered a tremendous drawback; at the climax, someone fired a cap pistol behind a spectator, intending to shock him. A startling climax! But I was afraid I might just startle someone into a heart attack. So for years I never performed the trick. Eventually, I decided that the trick was too good to pass up. So I simplified the handling and came up with this.

"This is the absolutely *true legend* of the demise of Wild Bill Hickock." Give the group a few seconds to grasp the incongruity of your statement. "Wild Bill was playing cards one day when he was dealt a hand that since has become quite notorious. Anybody know the hand?"

Somebody might. In any case, continue: "It was aces and eights. A pair of aces, a pair of eights, and a queen on the side. And, to this day, it's called, 'the dead man's hand.' Here, I'll get out the exact hand."

Hold the deck face up and fan through the cards. You will be removing these five and tossing them face up onto the table: ace of clubs, ace of diamonds, eight of hearts, eight of spades, and queen of hearts. These five cards will be dropped well forward on the table. In the process of removing them, you are going to drop several small face-up piles onto the table. These will be quite close to you. Start by fanning off five cards and dropping them face up onto the table. If one of the cards you're seeking is among the first five, take it out first and place it well forward of where you'll be forming your piles.

Continue fanning. Drop another pile of five cards to the left of the first pile. Drop a pile of six cards to the left of this. Meanwhile, continue removing the cards which constitute "the dead man's hand." As you go on through the deck, make other small piles, dropping them to the left of previous piles. Eventually, you'll have six or seven small piles in front of you and, perhaps, several cards left in your hand. "The dead man's hand" will be well forward of these piles.

As you fan through the cards, call no attention to the fact that you're making piles. Instead, discuss the specific cards you're looking for. After all five cards are removed from the deck, call attention to their values. It's important that spectators know exactly which cards are involved. You might say, "Notice that we have the ace of diamonds, normally a card that brings good luck. And certainly the ace of clubs doesn't have a bad reputation. Here's the queen of hearts. Her sister, the queen of spades, is a *terrible* card, but the queen of hearts stands for love. And what harm could there possibly be in the eight of hearts and the eight of spades? Nevertheless, collectively, these five cards are thought to be evil."

Jeff enjoys playing poker, so ask him to pick up "the dead man's hand."

"Look the cards over carefully, Jeff, and then pick out one of them that you like and set the other four onto the table. You'll have to remember the card you pick."

As you're talking, gather up the piles from left to right. Pick up the pile on your extreme left, turn it over, and place it in your hand. Do the same with the pile to the right of it. Gather up all but the last three piles. As you recall, one contains six cards and the other two contain five cards each— for a total of 16 cards.

Hold out the face-down cards you're holding. "Put your card here, Jeff." He places it on top. You casually gather up the remaining three piles any which way and place them on top of all. (The card Jeff selected is now 17th from the top.) Remaining on the table are the four other cards from "the dead man's hand." Pick these up and place them face down on top of the deck. (Jeff's selection is now 21st from the top.)

"Let's mix these up a bit. We'll use the old-time Western cut." You perform the *Roll-Up Cut* (refer to page 15), a false cut I designed specifically for this trick.

"What we're discussing here is Wild Bill." You now spell out the word *wild,* dealing out four cards in a row, one card for each letter. You deal from left to right, saying, "Wild, W-I-L-D." Next you spell *Bill,* dealing the next four cards on top of those on the table, and again going from left to right. "Bill, B-I-L-L."

Explain, "We're also discussing 'the dead man's hand.' " In the same way as described, deal out four cards for each of these words as you spell them: *dead, man's, hand.*

You now have four piles, each containing five cards. The bottom card of each pile is from "the dead man's hand."

Pick off the top card of those you're holding. "Jeff, you chose one card from 'the dead man's hand.' What was the name of that card?" He names it. You turn over the card; it's the one he chose. Drop the card face up in front of him.

Gather up the piles on the table in any order, placing one on top of the other. Put the combined pile on top of the deck.

"Jeff, let's assume that you're Wild Bill Hickock. There you sit with your back to the door. Could history repeat itself? Could you possibly get aces and eights? And if you do . . . Well, we'd better not discuss that.

"I'm going to deal out five hands in a minute. The fifth hand will go to me. Which one do you think Wild Bill would get—the first, second, third, or fourth?"

As you say "first," you deal a card to your left. As you say "second," you deal a card to the right of this. As you say "third," you remove the next card from the deck and hold it. Then you complete the question.

Whatever Jeff answers, you subtract the indicated number from 5. If Jeff answers "second," for instance, you subtract

2 from 5, giving you 3. This means that 3 cards must go to the bottom of the deck. Drop the card from your hand onto the table. Push together the 3 cards on the table and place the deck on top of them.

Suppose Jeff chooses "third." Subtract 3 from 5, getting 2. So 2 cards must go to the bottom of the deck. Place the card in your hand back on top of the deck. Drop the deck on top of the other two.

"Second" and "third" are the most common choices. If Jeff should say "first," you know that 4 cards must go to the bottom of the deck. You'll have to drop the card from your hand onto the table and deal down an additional card in the fourth position. All are pushed together, and the deck is dropped on top.

If Jeff should choose "fourth," you know that only one card goes to the bottom of the deck. Put the card in your hand back on top of the deck. Pick up one of the cards on the table and put it on top of the deck. Provide a bit of "time misdirection" by making a comment, like, "I'd sure hate to be in your boots, Wild Bill." Then drop the deck onto the remaining card on the table.

Once more you perform the *Roll-Up Cut* (refer to page 15). Address Jeff: "You already have one card, Wild Bill. Let's see how you do." Deal out *five* hands of four cards each. As you deal each round, count aloud, "One, two, three, four, five." Each time, place the appropriate card in front of Jeff. Gather up the other hands. Have Jeff turn over his cards one by one. As he turns each one, name it, increasing your intensity each time. When he names the last one, say, "I can't believe it. History has repeated itself."

It's at this point that the cap pistol was fired behind the spectator. I've never included this as part of the trick, and I do not encourage you to do so. Oh, all right, once in a while, I'll yell, "BAM!" But not *too* loud.

I prefer this ending: Look over Jeff's shoulder and say, "Hey, put down that rifle!" If Jeff turns, fine. If he doesn't, add, "Just kidding, Jeff. It's a revolver."

FUN

♣ ♦ ♥ ♠

♦ *The Arrangement* ♦

Now I give you a stunt which requires no skill whatever. Nevertheless, it is quite puzzling and amusing, and—in my version—provides plenty of spectator participation.

The only preparation is to have this written on the back of a business card or a piece of paper: 6S, 10S, 5C, 8C, 4S, JH, 3D, 7H, 2H, 9D, AD.

Let's say you're performing for a group of six. Say, "I'd like to show you a truly astonishing stunt. But I need to have certain cards. I hope that you'll all help me out." Give each person a pile of cards until the entire deck is distributed. "Please fan out the cards so that you can see the faces."

Take your list out and hold it in your left hand so that you can read it. Extend your right hand, palm up. The first card on your list is 6S (six of spades), so you say, "Who has the six of spades?" Go to the person who has it. Hold out your right hand. "Put it face down right here, please."

Look at the next card on the list. "Who has the ten of spades?" Go to that person and have him place that card face down on top of the first one.

Continue through the rest of the cards on the list, having the cards placed face down on your hand in order. As you do this, you are hopping back and forth, of course. After collecting the last card, put your list away. Stand there, panting. "I'm exhausted! I may be too tired to do this stunt." Pause. "Hold the applause."

Have the remaining cards gathered and set aside. Then have three different persons give your packet a complete cut.

Fan through the packet, faces towards yourself, saying, "All I have to do is find a certain card, and this is bound to work." Cut the cards so that the ace of diamonds becomes the top card. Turn the packet face down.

"Let's start by dealing the cards in order." Deal the top card face up onto the table, saying, "Ace." Put the next card on the bottom of the packet. Deal the next card face up on top of the ace, saying, "Two." Put the next card on the bottom of the packet. Continue all the way through the jack. Pick up the pile and turn it face down.

"Next, let's deal out all the odd cards, and then all the even cards." Deal the first card face up onto the table, saying, "Odd." Put the next card on the bottom of the packet. Deal the next card face up on top of the first one, again saying, "Odd." Continue this way until you deal out the jack of hearts. *Place the next card on the bottom* and deal out the next one face up, saying, "Even." Continue through the rest of the cards. Pick up the pile and turn it face down.

"Now, let's alternate the reds and the blacks." Go through the same procedure, announcing the color as each card is placed on the pile face up. Pick up the pile and turn it face down.

"That was fun. But we haven't done all red and then all black. Let's try it." Again, announce the colors as you go through the procedure. Pick up the pile and turn it face down.

Look puzzled. "I can't remember how we started out." If no one else can remember either, say, "Oh, yes, we did the cards in order, from ace to jack."

Go through the original procedure again.

As you gather up the cards, say, "Thank you so much. I couldn't have done it without you."

♦ *Lucky 13* ♦

Playing around with the cards one day, a new concept occurred to me. It took me a while to put a trick to it. What I finally developed has provided me, and spectators, with a lot of fun.

Reuben agrees to assist you. Say to him, "Most people believe that the number 13 is bad luck. But for me, it's always been good luck. Let me demonstrate. Reuben, I'm going to show you 13 cards. But first, I want you to think of a number from 1 to 13—not too high and not too low. Do you have one? Okay. Now I'd like you to notice what card lies at that number. Please don't stop me until we've done all 13 cards."

Take off the top card and show it to Reuben, saying, "One." Drop the card face down onto the table. Show the second card, saying, "Two." Drop this card face down onto the first card. Continue through 13 cards. Set the deck aside for the moment.

"Do you have your card? Good. Let me see if I can figure out what it is." Concentrate briefly. "No, it isn't coming to me. Maybe it'll help if you tell me the number you thought of."

Let's say that Reuben says 8. "So your card is 8 from the bottom. 8 from 13 is 5." Pick up the packet. Deal off four cards into a face-down pile, reciting the numbers 1 through 4 as you do so. Lift off the next card, saying, "Five." Toss the card face down onto the table, forward of the others. Drop the remaining cards in your hand on top of the cards you just dealt off. Tap the single card you tossed onto the table, saying, "I'm going to try to discover the name of your card without once looking at its face." Avert your head as you pick up the card and drop it on top of the main deck. Pick up the packet on the table and put it on top of the deck.

The chosen card is now on top of the deck. Tap the top card. "Right here is a magical card. This card will help me figure out what your card is." Lift off the card and study it, making sure no one else can see its face. Suppose the card is the three of clubs. Say hesitantly, "This tells me that your card is . . . black." Stall around. Eventually reveal that the card tells you that the suit is clubs. Grimace as you once more stare at the face of the card. "This magical card tells me that your card is . . . an eight . . . No! . . . a three. Your card is the three of clubs. Right?"

Right.

"Boy, I *love* this magical card!" Toss it onto the table face up.

Note: This trick works because most people have never had occasion to consider the actual mathematics involved. Let's take our example with Reuben; in the pile of 13 cards, you have a particular card at the 8th position from the bottom. What is its number from the top?

To the vast majority of spectators, it seems logical to subtract 8 from 13 to get the proper number. You certainly don't provide any time to think about it. But the actual number from the top is 6, not 5. And that, of course, is the basis of this trick. Suppose the particular card is at the 5th position from the bottom; the number from the top is 9, not 8, and so on.

If someone does catch on, it doesn't matter much with this particular trick.

◆ *The Black Card* ◆

Dressing up old tricks doesn't always work, but sometimes you end up with something infinitely better. As far as I'm concerned, this is what Wally Wilson accomplished with his comical version of this classic.

Preparation: Take out all the red cards from the deck and place them on top. Place a single black card 15th from the top. Now, let the miracles begin!

"I'm prepared to make a startling prediction," you announce. "Does anyone have a pencil and paper?" Pause. "All right then, I'm not *prepared* to make a startling prediction. Nevertheless . . ." Ah, you find a pencil and paper in your pocket. "Here. I'll write my prediction." Apparently, you jot down something on the paper. You fold the paper and set it aside.

"Gena, will you please assist me." She will.

Set the deck on the table. "Kindly cut off several cards." Make sure the packet she cuts off contains no more than 13 cards. Immediately look away. "I don't want to know the number. Hide them for right now."

Pick up the deck and begin dealing the cards face down, overlapping them. Deal towards Gena. Arrange to reach the edge of the table as you deal down the 14th card (Illus. 31). Say with a chuckle, "I guess that's enough."

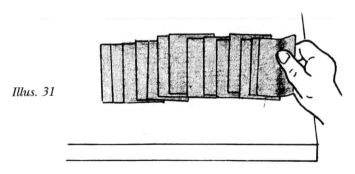

Illus. 31

Ask Gena to bring forth the little packet of cards she cut off. "I'd like you to count those cards, Gena, and then count to that same number in this row. For instance, if you cut off four cards, you'd count to the fourth card in the row. You'll start your count here." Touch the card closest to Gena.

She counts her cards and then counts to that same number in the row. Unknown to her, she has landed on the only black card among the reds. Have her remove it from the row and turn it face up. Let's suppose the card is the six of spades.

"Good! The six of spades. Please open my prediction and read it, Gena."

She opens it, but there's nothing to read. You only pretended to write something on the paper. "It says six of spades, doesn't it?"

Gena expresses confusion or denies that there's anything on the paper. "Oh, Gena. Apparently you don't believe in magic." Take the paper from her and hold it up so that all can see that it's blank. "I didn't write it really *hard*, but I'm sure some of you can read it. Surely someone here believes in magic. See? Six of spades." Single out a spectator, saying, "You can read it, can't you?"

Whatever the answer, say, "I can see that some of you doubt my powers to predict. And *you're* one of the doubters, Gena. I'm really surprised, especially after all we've been through together." Shake your head. "I guess I'll have to prove that I knew the card you'd choose. You picked a *black* card, Gena. Take a look at these." Turn over the cards you dealt out. "See? They're all red." Turn over the cards she cut off; they're red also. "So, you see, Gena, you picked the only black card among all the reds."

◆ *I Didn't Know* ◆

Here we have an extremely deceptive trick. I have placed it in the *Fun* category because it's so much fun to do. Complete success depends on how good an actor you are.

You need to know the top card of the deck. But spectators must not suspect this. As you gather up cards from a previous trick, you might make sure you get a known card on top. Or, again while gathering cards up, you might notice the bottom card. Then earnestly discuss the previous trick with spectators as you perform a casual overhand shuffle. You shuffle the last few cards singly, thus bringing the bottom card to the top. Done properly, it should appear that you're merely finding something for your hands to do as you converse.

Set the cards down and ask Scott to assist you. He's the perfect choice, since he's anxious to please and will follow instructions exactly. "Scott, I'd like you to cut off a small packet of cards from the top of the deck—somewhere in the neighborhood of 10 to 20." Turn away. "Now please think of a number from 1 to 10. Do you have one? Good. Now move that number of cards from the top of your packet to the bottom, one by one. Do this very quietly. Let me know when you're done."

When Scott says he's done, turn back and take the packet from him. "Do you know how many cards are here, Scott?"

He does not.

"Let's find out." Count them aloud, either into your hand, taking one on top of the other, or onto the table; the important thing is that you reverse the order. Let's suppose the number is 12. "So, Scott, we have 12 cards here. And there's no way I could possibly know which one of these is your chosen card." Place roughly half the packet in each hand. "Now which one of these packets do you think contains your card?" Put the packets back together so that they are in the same order as they were after you counted.

Somewhere along the line, Scott interrupts you to say something like, "But I don't *have* a card."

Here's where the acting ability comes in. "You didn't look at a card?" Pause. "Well, that's okay. You *did* think of a number though, right?" Right.

Hand Scott the packet. "When I turn away, move that number of cards from the top of your packet to the bottom, one by one." Turn away and provide these additional directions: "Now look at your bottom card and remember it." Pause. "Have you done that? Good. Let's see now . . . Have you shuffled the cards?" He hasn't. "Might as well give them a little shuffle."

This shuffle really throws everyone off—including magicians. In fact, you might as well have Scott give the cards *another* shuffle. At this point, you could read Scott's mind, since the card he looked at is the original top card which you peeked at. There's nothing wrong with doing this. A reasonably intelligent person will know, however, that you had some way of knowing the card in advance.

So, with a more sophisticated group, you might want to take the packet from Scott and go through the cards, studying them carefully. Finally, remove the chosen card (the original top card of the deck), and place it face down on the table. Scott names his card and then turns your choice over. Now when spectators wonder how you could have done it, they are faced with many more possibilities, and the real method is totally obscured. Just another one of your many miracles.

MISCELLANEOUS

♦ *I Guess So* ♦

Wouldn't it be wonderful if you could tell exactly how many cards a spectator cuts from the deck? Of course. But surely it would take years of practice. Yes. *Unless* you're willing to resort to treachery and deceit. Certainly *I* am.

I derived this trick from one by Norman Houghton, which required a trick deck. My method can be done impromptu with any deck. But it must be a complete deck of 52 cards.

Ask Lauren to shuffle the deck. Take the cards back. Hold them face down as you begin fanning them from hand to hand. Count the cards in groups of three as you fan them. When you have fanned out 12 cards, push one more into the right hand. Hold this packet of 13 separate from the rest as you continue slowly fanning the cards. Say to Lauren, "I'd like you to take any three cards from the deck. It doesn't matter which three you take. As you'll see, these are just 'confusion cards.' " Make sure she takes the cards from below your packet of 13.

"The values don't matter," you say. "Just set the three cards face down onto the table." While saying this, close up the deck. But with the tip of your left little finger get a small break below the 13 cards.

Grasp the deck from above with the right hand, transferring the break to the right thumb (Illus. 32). Casually, with your left thumb, riffle down a dozen or so cards on the left side of the deck (Illus. 33). With your right hand, lift off the 13-card packet and hand it to Lauren. "Shuffle these, will you, Lauren?"

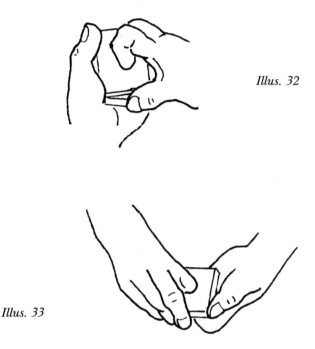

Illus. 32

Illus. 33

Since Bret isn't busy, hand him the rest of the deck. "And you might as well shuffle these, Bret."

Have Lauren set her pile onto the table. When Bret is done shuffling, have him set his pile down also. "Bret, would you cut some cards off that pile that you just shuffled and set them down on the table."

The situation: Three piles are on the table. One pile contains 13 cards, and you know which one. Three other cards are face down on the table.

"Lauren, I'd like you to place the 'confusion cards' on any piles you wish. Place them all on one pile, or two on one pile and one on another, or one on each pile—whatever you want."

These really *are* "confusion cards." You're using them to confuse the spectators as to what you're really up to.

It doesn't matter where Lauren places the three cards. All you have to do is keep track of the original pile of 13 cards. If Lauren adds cards to it, remember the new number.

"Over the years, I've developed some skill at estimating the number of cards in a pile. Let me show you what I mean. Bret, pick any one of the three piles."

If Bret chooses the first pile you handed out, simply stare at the pile for a few seconds and then say, "The pile contains exactly 13 cards." Or name the new number if Lauren added any cards to it. Have either of your assistants check the count. Gather up the cards and proceed to something else.

If, however, Bret chooses one of the other two piles, have him pick it up. "I'd like to demonstrate something. Bret, would you please count those out." He counts them aloud. "Now do you see how long that took?" Hold out your two hands palm up and flat. Have Lauren place one of the remaining piles on your right hand and Bret place the other remaining pile on your left hand (Illus. 34). You eye the two piles, and then give your estimate for each pile. "In this hand, I have (so many), and in this hand I have (so many)." Be sure to repeat your estimate. When Lauren and Bret count the piles, they discover that you were exactly right.

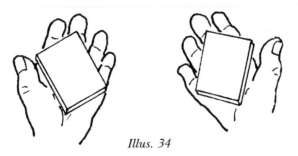

Illus. 34

Let's assume that in your right hand is the original pile you handed out, the one containing 13 cards. Further, let's assume that Lauren added one of the "confusion cards" to this pile. You know that the pile now contains 14 cards.

When Bret counted his selected pile aloud, he came up with, say, 21 cards. You add 21 to 14, getting 35. So the cards on the table and the cards in your right hand add up to 35. There are 52 cards in a full deck. Clearly, you subtract 35 from 52 to get the number of cards in your left hand—17. You need not be a lightning mathematician. Most of the figuring can be done as you stare at the piles resting on your palms, ostensibly trying to make an accurate estimate.

◆ *Oily Water* ◆

There are probably more four-ace tricks published than any other type. I would guess that a close second would be the old-time trick "Oil and Water." The reason for the title is that oil and water don't mix, and neither do red and black cards. No matter how you mix them, black cards gather together, and so do red cards. Every version I've come across requires a fair amount of sleight of hand. My version depends on a swindle and bare-faced lying.

Hand the deck to a spectator, saying, "Please remove four red cards and four black cards from the deck. Then arrange them so that they alternate black and red." The rest of the deck is set aside.

Take the eight cards from the spectator and fan them out face up, showing the alternating order. "You've probably heard the ridiculous theory that oil and water don't mix. Here we have red and black cards alternating. The black cards are oil, and the red cards are water. As you notice, they certainly do mix."

Turn the packet face down. "What happens if I move one card to the bottom?" Move the top card to the bottom. Turn the packet face up and fan it out. "Nothing. The cards still alternate." Turn the packet face down.

"How about two cards?" Move two cards to the bottom, one at a time. Turn the packet face up and fan it out. "They still alternate." Turn the packet face down.

"How about this?" Lift off two cards from the top, hold them to one side so that all can see that there are two, and then place them together on the bottom. Again turn the packet face up and fan it out. "Same thing." Turn the packet face down.

"What if I deal off a bunch of cards?" Take off five cards

with the right hand, dealing them one at a time and one on top of the other. Do *not* count them aloud. Place this bunch on the bottom of the packet. Turn the packet face up and show it, as before.

Still holding the packet face up, say, "What happens if I remove a pair together from this group?" Pull two cards out. "Obviously, I always get a red and a black. And notice that the *remaining* cards still alternate red and black."

Replace the two cards in their original position. Pull out another pair, again demonstrating that a pair taken together from anywhere in the group will consist of a red and black. Again, point out that the remaining cards alternate red and black. Replace this pair in their original position. "So, obviously, oil and water *do* mix."

Turn the packet face down. "Now a little demonstration." Take off *four* cards with the right hand, dealing them one at a time and one on top of the other. Don't count them aloud. Casually fan out the group so that all can see that it consists of alternate colors. Place this bunch face down on the bottom of the packet. "What happens when we deal off a bunch of cards? You know the answer." Make a motion as though to turn the packet over.

"Does it matter if we transfer them one at a time?" Move three, one at a time, from the top to the bottom. "Of course not." Take off the top two cards together and place them face down onto the table at your left. "And here's a pair of red and black."

Move two cards, one at a time, from the top to the bottom. Take off the top two cards together and place them face down onto the table at your right. "Another pair of red and black."

Move one card from the top to the bottom. Take off the top two cards together and place them face down onto the two at your *right*. "Another black and red pair." Drop the last pair onto the pair at your left. "And the last pair of red and black.

"So here we have proof positive . . ." Turn over the pile on the left and spread out the cards. Turn over the pile on the right and spread these out. "Hmm . . . Don't tell me that everybody else is right . . . that oil and water *don't* mix."

♦ *More Oily Water* ♦

T.S. Ransom adapted an old principle to the "oil and water" theme. I have added the ideas I developed in *Oily Water*. The trick may be done separately, but let's assume you're doing it as a follow-up to *Oily Water*.

"Let's try that again," you say, still skeptical. "First, we alternate the colors." Hold the four reds in a face-up packet in the left hand and the four blacks in a face-up packet in the right hand. Thumb off the card at the face of each packet so that it falls face up onto the table. On your right, a black card lies face up on the table; on your left, a red card lies face up on the table. Cross your hands so that the left hand can thumb off a card onto the card on the right, and vice versa (Illus. 35). Uncross your hands. Thumb off a card from each hand onto the piles where you started. Cross your hands and thumb off a card from each hand, as before.

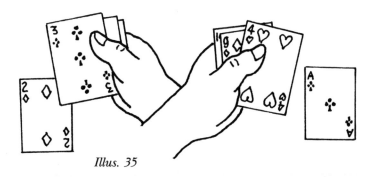

Illus. 35

Clearly, each pile alternates red and black cards. Place either pile on top of the other. Pick the combined pile up and turn it face down. Apparently, the packet alternates reds and blacks. Actually, the 4th and 5th cards from the top are of the same color.

You now go through the same procedure as in *Oily Water,* except that you do not count off the four cards at the beginning. Fill in with appropriate patter as you proceed:

Move three, one at a time, from the top to the bottom. Take off the top pair and place them face down onto the table at your left, saying, "A pair of red and black."

Move two cards, one at a time, from the top to the bottom. Take off the top pair and place them face down onto the table at your right. "Another pair of red and black."

Move one card from the top to the bottom. Take off the top pair and place them face down onto the pair at your right. "Another black and red pair." Drop the last pair onto the pair at your left. "And the last pair of red and black.

"*Now,* let's take a look." Show that each pile consists of the same color. Shake your head. "I guess I'm just not a good mixer."

♦ *Most Oily Water* ♦

In this final "oil and water" demonstration, we have another T.S. Ransom idea. I have changed it slightly to make it less obvious.

Feeling brave? This swindle works perfectly when done rapidly and with aplomb. If, however, you feel less than confident, don't bother trying it.

This works best as a follow-up to the previous trick, *More Oily Water.*

Turn the four red cards face down and hold them in the left hand. Turn the four black cards face down and take them in the right hand.

Now proceed rapidly! Cross your left hand over your right and thumb off each top card face down onto the table. (This is the same as Illus. 31, except that the cards are face down.) Uncross your hands. *Immediately* cross your right hand over your left and thumb each top card onto the card already there. Uncross your hands. Repeat your first move, in which you placed your left hand over your right. You now have three cards of the same color in each pile, and you are holding one card in each hand. As you uncross your hands this last time, turn the two cards face up. One is red and the other is black. Take them in one hand and proudly display them, saying, "See? Oil and water *do* mix."

Toss the two cards to one side. In eager anticipation, turn the three-card piles over. Each pile contains the same color. Shake your head ruefully. "Or not!"

◆ *Big Turnover* ◆

A card is chosen. The magician causes it to turn face up in the middle of the deck. This is one of the strongest tricks you can perform. Tom Ogden developed a patter theme, which makes the trick even more entertaining. I have expanded on the theme somewhat.

Fan through the deck, asking Troy to choose a card. When he returns the card to the deck, fan one card on top of it. Get a small break with your left little finger at this point. The chosen card is now the second card below the break. Perform one of the moves listed under *Control* (starting on page 8). The selected card is now second from the top of the deck.

"Troy, I will now magically cause your card to turn face up in the deck."

Tap the top of the deck. Tip the deck down so that all can see as you fan through the face-down cards. Clearly, no card is face up.

"But it may take a minute. I know what I did wrong. I should have riffled the cards." Riffle the ends of the deck. Fan through the cards as before. Again, failure.

"Okay, Troy, then I'll do it the easy way." Tap the top card. "I'll just turn your chosen card over . . . like this!"

Grasp the top card at the outer end with your right hand and turn it over so that you're holding it a few inches to the right of the deck. As you do this, push off the next card slightly with your left thumb. As you draw this card back onto the deck with your left thumb, get a small break beneath it with your left little finger. Immediately place the face-up card in your right hand squarely on top of it.

The situation: You have a face-up card on top of the deck. Beneath it is the chosen card. And below this card, you're holding a small break with your left little finger.

As you place the card face up onto the deck, say, "That *is* your card, isn't it, Troy?"

No, it isn't.

With your right hand, lift off the top two cards as though they are one. Your first finger rests on top, the other fingers are at the outer end, and the thumb is at the inner end (Illus. 36). With your left thumb, flip over the remainder of the deck so that it is face up. Slide the double-card under the deck as though you are replacing the face-up card on top (Illus. 37). Raise the right first finger to facilitate the placement.

2 cards are held as one.

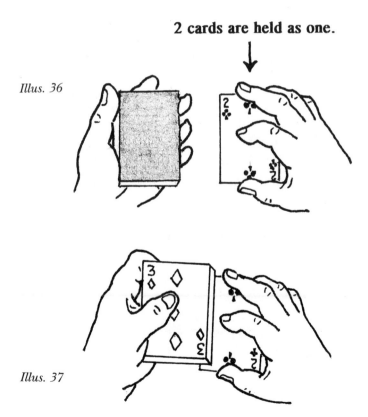

Illus. 36

Illus. 37

The entire deck is now face up, except for the chosen card, which is face down at the rear of the deck. Since the deck is apparently face up, it's perfectly logical for you to say, "Now I *know* that your card is face up. It *has* to be one of these face-up cards." Tip the cards down and fan through about half of the face-up deck. Close up the cards and casually give them a cut. Turn the deck face down.

"See, Troy? I told you I'd turn your card face up." To the rest of the group: "Thank you so much. I hope you enjoyed that little demonstration."

Pause, looking slightly angry. "Did I hear someone say the word 'putrid'?" Since Francine is very good-natured, you turn to her, saying, "Was that you, Francine?" Don't give her a chance to answer. "Shame on you. Do you think it's easy doing magic? Let's see you give it a try."

Make her take the deck. "What was your card, Troy?" He names it.

"All right, Francine, let's see *you* be magic. Tap the top card of the deck and then fan through the cards."

She does. And, of course, the chosen card is face up.

"Good heavens! She got it!" Pause briefly. "You know, Francine, I could really use a good assistant . . ."

♦ *Easy Match* ♦

Simple is good. In this instance, simple is not only good, but extremely deceptive. This fine trick by Cy Keller has fooled some of the best.

The original trick called for two decks. I have arranged a one-deck version which is totally impromptu.

Rex will be delighted to assist you. "In this experiment, Rex," you say, "we'll each need about half the cards." Turn the deck faces towards you and note the bottom card. You're going to fan through the deck, looking for its mate—the card that matches it in color and value. Fan through several cards and place them *face down* in front of yourself, saying, "Some for me." Fan through several more. If the mate is not in sight, place these cards face down on your pile, saying, "Some more for me."

Fan through to the mate of the original bottom card. Lift off this batch, including the mate. Even up the group and place it *face up* in front of Rex, saying, "And some for you." You now have a small face-down packet in front of you, the bottom card of this pile being the original bottom card. In front of Rex is a face-up pile; the lowermost card is the mate to your bottom card.

If the pile in front of Rex is fairly small, add cards from the deck to his pile and to yours until each consists of about half the deck. Naturally, the cards go on his pile face up and on yours face down. As you add cards to the piles, keep saying, "Some for you" and "Some for me."

If the pile in front of Rex is quite large, put the rest of the deck onto your pile. If his pile is still larger than yours, take some cards from his, turn them face down, and put them onto your pile.

It sounds a little complicated, but the bottom line is this:

Once you've put down the first two piles, you make sure that each consists of about half the deck.

Pick up your pile and casually give it an overhand shuffle as you tell Rex, "Please pick up your pile and turn it face down." Near the end of your overhand shuffle, draw off the last few cards singly, bringing the bottom card to the top. The top card of your pile now matches the top card of Rex's pile.

"Now for the experiment. Rex, let's see what happens when we perform the identical actions. Please do exactly what I do."

With Rex following your example with his cards, you cut off the top half of your packet. You place this top half face down onto the table. Turn the cards in your hand face up and give them several overhand shuffles (Illus. 38). Even up these cards and hold them face up in your left hand in the dealing position (Illus. 39). Lift off the top card of those you placed on the table and place this card face down on top of the face-up packet you're holding. Turn this packet face down and place it on top of your pile on the table. Rex, of course, has gone through the identical routine with his cards.

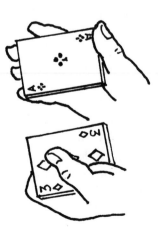

Illus. 38

Illus. 39

In case Rex and others are not sufficiently disoriented, you now use a bit of "time misdirection" so that they will forget precisely what has occurred. "Very often, Rex, when two persons perform identical actions, they get similar results. When this happens, some people call it coincidence, others call it fate. I think of it as good luck, especially if I'm conducting the experiment. So we performed the same actions; let's see the result."

Spread your cards out face down and have Rex do the same. His face-up card matches yours.

◆ *List to One Side* ◆

Time is hanging heavy on your hands. Why not telephone
Nola and perform a card trick for her?

All you need is a pencil and paper, along with enough
persuasive power to convince Nola to cooperate.

Start by asking her to get a deck of cards. When she returns
to the phone, ask her to shuffle the deck. Then: "Nola, deal
the cards from the top of the deck into a face-up pile. Please
name the cards as you deal them out."

As she names the cards, jot down the name of each one,
using this conventional shorthand:

9C

10S

JH

QD

(These stand for nine of clubs, ten of spades, jack of hearts,
and queen of diamonds.)

After Nola deals ten-plus cards, tell her that she can stop
whenever she wishes. Have her set the deck aside. "Pick out
any card you want from those you dealt off. Remember that
card and stick it into the middle of the main deck. Now shuffle up the main deck."

When she's ready, say, "Shuffle up the rest of the cards
that you dealt off and put them on top of the main deck.
When you're ready, give the deck a complete cut."

These are your final instructions: "Again, would you deal
the cards from the top into a face-up pile and name the cards
as you deal them." As she names the cards, keep your eye on
the card names you jotted down. As soon as she names one,

put a check mark by it. Continue checking off cards from the group. (Because she shuffled these cards, they will not be in order. But the checked-off cards *will* be together in a bunch.) Eventually, you will check off all the cards in the group except one. That is her chosen card. Stop Nola and tell her the name of her chosen card.

Sometimes the spectator will name a card from the group you wrote down but then will name cards that are *not* in the group. That first card she named from the group is her chosen card.

Note: When Nola names the cards for the second time, you might want to make a second list which you can use after she gets well down in the deck. This eliminates the possibility of your failing to check off one of the cards on your initial list.

Afterword

You're interested in card magic. Let's suppose you do all the right things. You learn a dozen really good card tricks. You practise them till you have them down perfectly. You toss in some superb, imaginative patter. Then you try them out on susceptible, trusting friends and relatives—with great success! Now what? Where do you go from here?

It depends on how interested you are. Do you aspire to become one of the all-time greats, or would you prefer to dabble in magic? Do you want to become a professional, or remain an amateur? Nothing wrong with any of these.

Obviously, if you plan to make money performing magic, you'd better be prepared to practise a great deal. Furthermore, you'd better be creative, because very few spectators are interested in stale patter or ordinary tricks. Are there jobs? Yes. Probably more jobs than ever before. But there are more magicians than ever before, too. So you'd better be good. And dedicated. Furthermore, you'd better realize that very few magicians make their living solely doing magic. Most have a full-time job and perform magic as a sideline.

On the other hand, being an amateur magician has its rewards. There is certainly less pressure. No one expects you to be as good as a professional, so when you do a trick especially well, you hear things like, "You're a regular professional." It's much more gratifying than being a professional and hearing the reverse. Also, as an amateur, you view magic as a hobby. You can devote as much time to it as you choose, attaining perfection in your own good time.

Whatever your aspirations, you should get together with fellow magicians. They are a surprisingly helpful and friendly lot. Check your phone book to see if there's a magic shop in your area. If so, you can drop in and get all the information you need about local organizations. Furthermore, you might just meet other magicians who can help you out with advice.

What if there is no magic shop in your area? Again, check the phone book. If any professional magicians are operating in your area, they will probably be listed. Feel free to give a call. Explain your situation and ask about any local group, formal or informal. Chances are, you'll get all the information you need about local magicians and organizations.

ABOUT THE AUTHOR

♣ ♦ ♥ ♠

Bob Longe, a retired English teacher, is an ardent hobbyist. He has charted stocks, played duplicate bridge, and painted. He plays the piano, the tenor banjo, and the ukulele. Inspired by the big stage shows of the great illusionists Blackstone and Dante, he took up magic in the 1930s. Early on, he wrote two booklets on card tricks: *The Invisible Deck* was published by the Ireland Magic Company of Chicago; *The Visible Deck* was self-published. Over the years, he has taught magic, particularly card tricks and coin tricks, to dozens of aspiring magicians.

In the late 1970s, Bob wrote, coproduced, and performed in the syndicated radio satire show "Steve Sado, Private Eye." He lives in Rochester Hills, Michigan, with his wife, Betty.

♦ *STERLING Books by Bob Longe* ♦

101 Amazing Card Tricks
Easy Card Tricks
Easy Magic Tricks
Great Card Tricks
Mind Reading Magic Tricks
Nutty Challenges & Zany Dares
World's Best Card Tricks
World's Best Coin Tricks
World's Greatest Card Tricks

MASTERY LEVELS
CHART & INDEX
♣ ♦ ♥ ♠